PRAISE

IF I DON'T LAUGH, I'LL CRY

"Molly Stillman's vibrant, funny voice shines through in her memoir, *If I Don't Laugh, I'll Cry*. Her story is ultimately uplifting and inspirational, with a happy ending that is both hard won and ferociously fought for. . . . Her message is clear and strong: through faith and family and Jesus, all things are possible."
—**KRISTIN HANNAH, #1 *NEW YORK TIMES* BESTSELLING AUTHOR**

"Thank goodness this class clown made it out of the classroom and into our literary world! In *If I Don't Laugh, I'll Cry* Molly does a fantastic job of not only inviting us into her life but making sure to welcome us with vulnerability and grace. By the time you reach the end, you just might find that you're exactly what you've been looking for."
—**TYLER MERRITT, AUTHOR OF *I TAKE MY COFFEE BLACK* AND CREATOR OF THE TYLER MERRITT PROJECT**

"Molly's journey and her retelling of it is full of both heartbreak and hope. It will inspire you to see your own life through a lens of redemption and possibility, while simultaneously reminding you to lighten up a bit and not be afraid to laugh at yourself every once in a while."
—**LIZ BOHANNON, FOUNDER OF SSEKO DESIGNS, AUTHOR OF *BEGINNER'S PLUCK*, AND HOST OF THE *PLUCKING UP* PODCAST**

"Through her incredible resilience, Molly Stillman teaches us that it's never too late to find faith, hope, and joy in the most unexpected circumstances. *If I Don't Laugh, I'll Cry* will empower you as you take the next steps in your personal journey."
—**BOLA SOKUNBI, FOUNDER AND CEO OF CLEVER GIRL FINANCE AND BESTSELLING AUTHOR OF THE CLEVER GIRL FINANCE SERIES AND *CHOOSING TO PROSPER***

"Being human is hard, and what we suffer on this side of heaven is often unbearable and unbelievable. Molly adds levity to our shared human experiences and offers comforting and practical insight. You'll want to get a copy of this book for everyone you know and love."
—**ASHLEY ABERCROMBIE, AUTHOR OF *RISE OF THE TRUTH TELLER* AND *LOVE IS THE RESISTANCE***

"I wept my way through the final chapter of Molly's book and laughed at its ending. Her story is a story for each of us: one of soul-jarring tragedy, bone-headed mistakes, aimless wandering—and the grace of a God whose relentless love meets us in the midst of it all. I hope you will read it and find that same grace and love waiting for you."
—**STEVE BEZNER, PASTOR OF HOUSTON NORTHWEST CHURCH**

"*If I Don't Laugh, I'll Cry* showcases Molly's humor and authenticity as she tells her amazing story of tears and triumph. . . . Her story of how God's grace gave her a life of freedom and love is one that everyone can relate to and will draw hope from. I can't wait for the world to read it!"

—COREY PAUL, BILLBOARD-CHARTING ARTIST, CEO OF 1M & CO., AND AUTHOR OF *PATH TO PODCAST SUCCESS*

"Living up to its title, *If I Don't Laugh, I'll Cry* is equal parts comedy, tragedy, coming of age, and coming to faith, all brilliantly bound up into one. . . . If you are looking for real hope and resilience to guide you through life's hardest trials, this book is also for you."

—SHARON HODDE MILLER, AUTHOR OF *THE COST OF CONTROL*

"*If I Don't Laugh, I'll Cry* is for the girl who has been told that she's 'too much' or the seeker who isn't sure that she will ever be 'Christian enough' for God to love. You have always been worthy. And Molly Stillman wants to make sure you know it."

—HEATHER THOMPSON DAY, AUTHOR OF *I'LL SEE YOU TOMORROW*

"This book will definitely make you laugh a little, see yourself in Molly's honest words, and leave you inspired to live a full life that honors God. I read it in one sitting and highly recommend it!"

—KRISTEN WELCH, BESTSELLING AUTHOR OF *RAISING GRATEFUL KIDS IN AN ENTITLED WORLD*

"Usually a memoir like this is written from old age, but Molly has lived one thousand lifetimes in her three decades and remembers so many delightful and haunting details that you'll be turning pages faster and faster to find out what happens."

—REBECCA SMITH, AUTHOR OF *A BETTER LIFE*

"Molly's unique ability to blend humor with heartfelt storytelling makes this memoir a delightful and inspiring read for anyone looking to find hope and purpose amid life's challenges."

—JESSICA HONEGGER, FOUNDER OF NOONDAY COLLECTION AND AUTHOR OF *IMPERFECT COURAGE*

"Molly has written with such vulnerability and tenderness that anyone who reads this book will be assured that they are not alone. If you begin reading the book in tears, you will finish it with laughter and a glimmer of joy. This book is a true gift!"

—DANIEL GROTHE, AUTHOR OF *CHASING WISDOM* AND *THE POWER OF PLACE*

"For all of us who have lived hard parts of our story, both by the things that have happened to us and the things we brought on ourselves, this is the anthem we've been waiting for—a permission slip to laugh again, to *live* again, and to finally forgive ourselves for taking the long way around."

—MARY MARANTZ, BESTSELLING AUTHOR OF *DIRT* AND *SLOW GROWTH EQUALS STRONG ROOTS* AND HOST OF *THE MARY MARANTZ SHOW*

if i don't laugh i'll cry

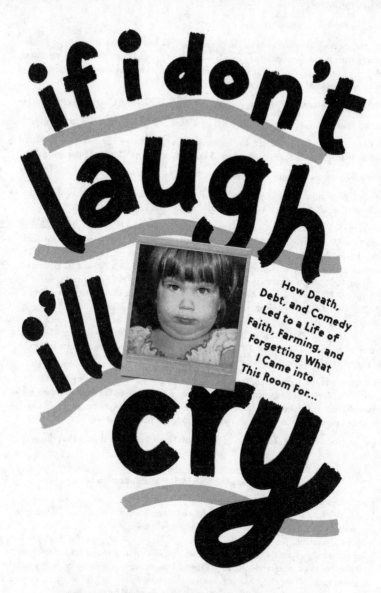

How Death,
Debt, and Comedy
Led to a Life of
Faith, Farming, and
Forgetting What
I Came into
This Room For...

Molly Stillman

NELSON
BOOKS

An Imprint of Thomas Nelson

If I Don't Laugh, I'll Cry

Excerpts from *Home Before Morning* are used with permission from Charles Thomas Buckley.

Excerpts from *Visions of War, Dreams of Peace* are used with permission from Joan Furey.

Published in Nashville, Tennessee, by Nelson Books, an imprint of Thomas Nelson. Nelson Books and Thomas Nelson are registered trademarks of HarperCollins Christian Publishing, Inc.

Published in association with Punchline Agency LLC.

Thomas Nelson titles may be purchased in bulk for educational, business, fundraising, or sales promotional use. For information, please email SpecialMarkets@ThomasNelson.com.

Unless otherwise noted, Scripture quotations are taken from The Holy Bible, New International Version®, NIV®. Copyright © 1973, 1978, 1984, 2011 by Biblica, Inc.® Used by permission of Zondervan. All rights reserved worldwide. www.Zondervan.com. The "NIV" and "New International Version" are trademarks registered in the United States Patent and Trademark Office by Biblica, Inc.® Scripture quotations marked CSB are taken from the Christian Standard Bible®. Copyright © 2017 by Holman Bible Publishers. Used by permission. Christian Standard Bible® and CSB® are federally registered trademarks of Holman Bible Publishers. Scripture quotations marked KJV are taken from the King James Version. Public Domain. Scripture quotations marked MSG are taken from THE MESSAGE. Copyright © 1993, 2002, 2018 by Eugene H. Peterson. Used by permission of NavPress. All rights reserved. Represented by Tyndale House Publishers, a Division of Tyndale House Ministries.

Any internet addresses, phone numbers, or company or product information printed in this book are offered as a resource and are not intended in any way to be or to imply an endorsement by Thomas Nelson, nor does Thomas Nelson vouch for the existence, content, or services of these sites, phone numbers, companies, or products beyond the life of this book.

Names and identifying characteristics of some individuals have been changed to preserve their privacy.

Library of Congress Cataloging-in-Publication Data

Names: Stillman, Molly, 1985- author.
Title: If I don't laugh, I'll cry : how death, debt, and comedy led to a life of faith, farming, and forgetting what I came into this room for / Molly Stillman.
Description: Nashville, Tennessee : Nelson Books, [2024] | Summary: "In this laugh-out-loud and heartfelt memoir, writer, speaker, and podcaster Molly Stillman shares her unforgettable story of losing her mother, squandering an unexpected quarter-of-a-million-dollar inheritance in less than two years, attempting to launch a career in comedy but ending up on a farm instead, and finding faith, hope, and joy in the middle of it all"-- Provided by publisher.
Identifiers: LCCN 2023045383 (print) | LCCN 2023045384 (ebook) | ISBN 9781400243273 (trade paperback) | ISBN 9781400243204 (ebook)
Subjects: LCSH: Resilience (Personality trait)--Religious aspects--Christianity. | Inheritance and succession. | Debt.
Classification: LCC BF698.35.R47 S755 2024 (print) | LCC BF698.35.R47 (ebook) | DDC 155.2/4--dc23/eng/20231130
LC record available at https://lccn.loc.gov/2023045383
LC ebook record available at https://lccn.loc.gov/2023045384

Printed in the United States of America

24 25 26 27 28 LBC 5 4 3 2 1

For my dad.

And for the guys who work at my local Circle K, thanks for always making sure the fountain Diet Coke is working for me.

CONTENTS

CONTENTS

FOREWORD

There are moments in life that happen so unexpectedly and shine so brightly that it is impossible to believe they are random. One such moment happened when I met Molly Stillman.

A little back story: In 2023 I was gearing up for the launch of my novel about the American nurses who served in the Vietnam War. I had worked on the novel for three years but had been imagining it for almost two decades.

What took me so long, you ask? Truth be told, I was afraid to tackle such an important subject. I knew it would take everything I had to recreate the turbulent Vietnam era of my youth, and for years I worried that I was too young and not a good enough writer.

I was a kid during the war, and I remember the turbulence of the time well. My best friend's father was shot down and lost. I put on a silver prisoner-of-war bracelet for him when I was eleven years old. He never came home. When the war ended, I saw how the returning Vietnam veterans were treated. All of it made a lasting impression on me and fueled my desire to tell a story about this divided time in America.

But what story? It wasn't until we were in the middle of a world-wide pandemic and I saw how exhausted and overworked our nurses and doctors were that it all came to together for me and clicked in my head.

The nurses. *The Women.*

It was then, in the years of lockdown and panic and fear, that I began my novel about the brave, resilient young women—mostly nurses, but not all—who served in the Vietnam War. In doing the research and the writing, I met and spoke with several nurses who had served. Everyone I spoke to knew and mentioned Molly's mother, Lynda Van Devanter, and her searing memoir, *Home Before Morning.* Over the course of the writing, I began to feel that I knew these women. Certainly I loved and admired them. It was so important to me that I do justice to their service.

By the summer of 2023, *The Women* was slowly being revealed to the world. I had begun to post a few photos and snippets on my social media—Instagram and Facebook. Now, I am no social media dynamo and hardly know how it all works. But one day I was watching television with my husband, and my phone was beside me charging. A social media alert came through. Ordinarily I wouldn't even look at such a thing and it would be lost. On this evening, however, I glanced at it and saw the words "I'm Molly, Lynda Van Devanter's daughter" flash across the front of my phone.

I immediately reached out to Molly and sent her a copy of my novel, and afterward we talked. And talked. And talked.

At first it was about the book and Vietnam and Molly's mother's incredible journey of healing after the war, but then we moved on to what we have in common, the pain and grief we share. Like Molly, I lost my mother when I was young. I know about going in search of your life without a mother to stand beside you and cheer you on. I know the pain of it, how it stays with you, how you find yourself crying at the oddest of times. There's a part of you that is simply missing, and you have to find a way to go on and become unbroken. That is Molly's journey in this book.

She dares to share herself and her story with readers, even when that story is messy or embarrassing or heartbreaking. While her loss and grief and fear shine through in this memoir, so do her humor and hope. She doesn't pull back; instead, she bares it all and tells the reader what worked for her, how finding Jesus and surrendering to her faith saved her spirit and made her whole again.

On Veteran's Day, 2023, I was honored to join the female veterans at the Vietnam Women's Memorial in Washington, DC, for the thirtieth anniversary of the memorial. It was awe-inspiring, heart-expanding, and heartbreaking to see these women gather, many of them for the first time in years, to share their stories and cry and laugh and hug.

And there was Molly at the podium for storytelling, standing proudly beside the memorial, talking about her mother's service, sharing both the heartbreaking and beautiful moments, bringing her tenacious mother beautifully back to life. I don't think there was a dry eye in the crowd.

I know that Molly's mom, Lynda, would be so proud of her daughter and this book. I'm sure Molly felt her mother's spirit often as she was writing. I know I still do.

Kristin Hannah
#1 *New York Times* bestselling
author of *The Nightingale* and
The Great Alone

AUTHOR'S NOTE*

Every event and story I share in the following pages is true and has been faithfully rendered as I best remember it. I've had conversations with others confirming details and have extensively researched personal journals, blog posts, home videos, and photo albums to fill in the gaps. In most cases, I've changed people's names or identifying details in stories and events in order to protect their privacy.

All of the conversations and dialogue throughout the book come from my own personal recollection. They are not written to represent word-for-word documentation and dialogue; rather, I have retold the conversations in a way that keeps the spirit and meaning of what was said.

At the end of the day, this is my story, and I'm gonna tell it the way I want.

---

* Ya know, as I was writing this note, I thought to myself, *Why are there such things as authors' notes to begin with? Like, isn't the *whole book* an author's note? Why would there need to be an "author's note" to the larger author's note? Would the author's note be better titled a "sidenote"?* Don't even get me started on footnotes or endnotes.

These are my notes about authors' notes.

Okay, on to the book now.

WELL, ALLOW ME TO MAKE YOUR ACQUAINTANCE

(THIS IS THE INTRODUCTION)

Question for you: Have you ever hung out with a group of people? Perhaps the group of people is a mix of old friends and new friends, or maybe said group is just a bunch of acquaintances. Or possibly it's one person you know and a whole bunch of people you don't. I want you, right now, to close your eyes and go to that place with those people in your mind.

Wait, don't close your eyes. That would be ridiculous because you're reading a book. Don't close your eyes, just . . . I don't know . . . mentally go there somehow, someway. Work with me.

Are you there now? Great.

Now that we've established you're with a group of people . . . let's pretend you are having a conversation with one or two or nine people during the course of the evening, and you say a bunch of human words. Doesn't matter what words. Doesn't even matter what language those words are spoken in. These are *your* words that come from *your* mouth. The words could be a story of your own that you find yourself telling; the words could be a response to someone else's story; the words could be some spicy political commentary, a hot take on some pop-culture reference, or even a dad joke . . . The content here is irrelevant. The point is, you have found yourself in a situation in which you are speaking words. And while you speak those words, the other people around you are listening to those words.

When the event ends, you leave and go home. Whether you bid a traditional farewell or make a French exit or an Irish goodbye*—it doesn't matter. You are gone. Peace. Outta there. But then, immediately upon leaving the premises, you proceed to replay the aforementioned conversations in your brain whilst overanalyzing every last word, guffaw, and utterance that came out of your mouth. You find yourself cringing at the sounds that left your mouth. You wonder why on earth you said this or responded with that. You briefly consider moving to the island of Malta because it would be easier than having to face those people ever again because what you said was just *that* embarrassing.

You will continue to repeat this cycle for the next 250 years (or until you die—whichever comes first). (That said, I haven't yet ruled out the fact that I may *still* continue the cycle while walking the gold streets of heaven.) Now look, I know that in the book of Revelation Jesus says that in heaven "he will wipe away every tear from their eyes. Death will be no more; grief, crying, and pain will be no more, because the previous things have passed away" (Revelation 21:4 CSB). But I don't see him mentioning anything about no more overanalyzing . . . Or shall we call it "deep reflection"?

---

* The Irish goodbye, also known as the French exit, is to depart from a place in secret, without saying goodbye to anyone. To disappear from an event without fanfare. To slip quietly into the night so as not to have to "make rounds." My ancestry.com DNA analysis tells me I'm 76 percent Irish, so I am fairly certain I was destined to excel at the Irish goodbye.

What I'm getting at is: Have you ever said something and *immediately* regretted it the moment the words exited your mouth? Are you constantly worrying about whether the people in the room even like you? Do you often wonder if you're "a bit much" for people?

Hi! It's me! Nice to meet you!

So riddle me this: If this is the plight with which I regularly struggle, why on God's green earth would I choose to write a full-on great American memoir made of my own human words that share, in detail, a whole lot of my personal junk? Why would I write a book in which I have the potential to put my foot in my mouth? Why would I write a book using words that will be printed for all of eternity (or however long this work stays actively in print)? Only for me to over-analyze it for the next 250 years?

Why would I do this to myself?

Your guess is as good as mine.

I guess part of it is, on a basic level, because I love books. Memoir, in particular, is my favorite genre because I'm nosy, and I like learning about other people's lives. I also oddly like to read about the lives of people who have been through incredibly hard things, so I can then close the book, sigh, and say, "Well, I guess my life's not so bad!" Then I head back to the kitchen to eat a piece of string cheese. Look, the Lord is still working on me, okay?

The other part is because I knew I was supposed to write this book.

I grew up dreaming of writing a book. My mom was a writer (much more on this to come), and I wanted to be just like her. I have this vivid memory of being five years old and watching my mom sitting at her typewriter, surrounded by stacks of papers, notes, and journals, working on her next writing project. I'd run downstairs to grab my Fisher-Price typewriter and haul it back up, then sit on the floor next to her, hunting and pecking each key in an attempt to write some transcendent story. I remember the first "book" I wrote, which never went to print. I was eight, and it was a children's book about a unicorn that had superpowers. It was titled *Supercorn* because *obviously*.[†]

But then I got older. I wasn't a kid anymore, and life happened. Mom got sick. Things got hard. Really hard. I got depressed. My family struggled. I felt lost. We felt alone. Mom died. I made some really stupid decisions. I fumbled along, doing everything I could in my power to pull myself up by my nonexistent bootstraps. I wore a facade like a badge of honor, making it seem like I was doing "just fine" and that everything was "awesome."

Then I got some money. And I thought, *That'll fix it!* Then I lost all the money. And I thought, *Well, I broke it!* I was embarrassed, but mostly I was ashamed.

I spent my days trying to impress people and find identity in worldly success. I spent my nights onstage doing improvisational and sketch comedy—making stuff up and making people laugh. Comedy was what I was convinced I was born to do, and I was dead set on doing it.

On the outside, I looked fantastic. But underneath it all, I was miserable.

But God.

Wait, wait! If because I said "But God" makes you want to close this book, please don't. Hear me out.

There was a time, for quite a long time, when I genuinely thought that no longer living would be better than living. There was a time

---

† Come to think of it, a unicorn is already mythical, so that means it would already have superpowers because it's a unicorn. So a unicorn with superpowers is basically a double negative. Or a double positive? I don't know, I was today years old when this thought occurred to me.

when I thought every ounce of hope I had was lost. There was a time when I thought I was destined to be the next Molly Shannon or Tina Fey on *Saturday Night Live*. There was a time when I thought I would never be really, truly loved. There was a time when I thought no one would ever know the real me.

There was a time when I'd fallen flat on my proverbial face in the metaphorical mud and mire, when the God I'd shunned, the God I'd Heismaned, the God I'd ignored, the God I'd cursed leaned down, lifted my chin out of the muck, looked me in the eye, picked me up, set my feet upon a rock, gave me a firm place to stand, and said, "I got you." Then, in his kindness, he taught me what true love looks like, what true peace feels like, and where I can find the source of true joy. He put a new song in my mouth.

> I waited patiently for the LORD;
>> he turned to me and heard my cry.
> *He lifted me out of the slimy pit,*
>> *out of the mud and mire;*
> *he set my feet on a rock*
>> *and gave me a firm place to stand.*
> He put a new song in my mouth,
>> a hymn of praise to our God.
> Many will see and fear the LORD
>> and put their trust in him.
>
> PSALM 40:1-3 (EMPHASIS MINE)

And *everything* changed.

This book is that story.

Much like life, it's a messy story, it's a funny story, it's a sad story, and it's also an unfinished story. It's a story that, at one time, I went to great lengths to cover up. But now it's a story I've been called to steward well. And, whether I like it or not, it's a story I have to tell. (Oh! That rhymed!)

Now, as I just mentioned, I'm a chronic overanalyzer. And truth be told, I'm afraid you might hate my story, judge my story, or even be indifferent toward my story. I have come to terms with that. At the end of the day, my goal is to be faithful to God and the difficult task he's set before me.

I aim for every word you read to ultimately honor and glorify God—even the really muddy and messy parts. Because it's the muddy and messy parts that brought me to him. I've learned that God likes to use the muddy and messy for his glory. If at the end of this book you've laughed, you've cried, you've laughed 'til you cried, you've felt less alone, and you've learned even a little bit more about the Jesus I follow, then I've done my job.

Here we go.

1

WINDFALL

AUGUST 23, 2006

The more money we come across,
the more problems we see.

CHRISTOPHER GEORGE LATORE WALLACE

I think it's called an "out of money experience."

It is said, *by people who I assume know what they're talking about*, that about 70 percent of lottery winners go entirely broke within five years of receiving their winnings. In a way, I am a part of that statistic.

Let me set the stage for you: It was my twenty-first birthday. I'd just begun my senior year at Christopher Newport University in Newport News, Virginia. I was the quintessential student, bright-eyed and bushy-tailed, ready to take on my final year of college. I was at the peak of my young-adult game. I was president of the Student Government Association (SGA), I was in a sorority, I starred in the campus sketch comedy group, I was in multiple honor societies, I had a great boyfriend and an incredible group of friends.

For the summer, instead of going back to my hometown of Herndon, Virginia, I'd stayed in Newport News to waitress during

1

the day at a local crab shack that overlooked the James River. I lived in an on-campus apartment for juniors and seniors, and my boyfriend and a few sorority sisters had also stayed in town so we could hang out and go to Busch Gardens as much as humanly possible. It was one of the best summers of my life. I hadn't a care in the world.

The night before my twenty-first birthday, my friends and I went to a karaoke bar and restaurant. We waited for midnight to hit so everyone could buy me my first drinks as a twenty-one-year-old. Don't go getting any ideas; the evening was very tame—just me, Derek (my boyfriend), a couple of his friends, and a handful of my closest sorority sisters. Nothing to write home about, except for maybe the bring-the-house-down Lauryn Hill / Fugees rendition of "Killing Me Softly with His Song" that I belted out during karaoke.*

On the morning of my birthday, I woke up and headed from my apartment to the main campus across the street to grab breakfast and pop in to the SGA office. Part of my routine was to check in first thing in the morning to see if anything immediate or pressing needed my attention. (You see, I was very important; *people knew me*, my apartment smelled of rich mahogany, and I had many leather-bound books.)

A blinking red light on my desk phone indicated I had a new voicemail. The campus post office had called to let me know a certified letter that I needed to sign for was waiting for me in the mailroom. Having never been the recipient of a certified letter before, I didn't think much of it as I walked over to the mailroom to pick it up.

---

* Fun fact about me: "Killing Me Softly with His Song" has been, and always will be, my go-to karaoke song, no matter the time or place. When I get to that "whoaaaaaaaa oh oh ah ah ah ah" part (you know the one), I take flight. I am in my element. I have sung that song in many a karaoke bar around the country, and it slays every time—most notably in the summer of 2007, when for reasons I don't really remember, I was in a drag bar called Suite on the Upper West Side of Manhattan. I was a bona fide chanteuse with a hundred drag queens screaming my name while I sang. Quite a scene from a bygone era of my life.

"Good morning, Carol!" I said to the campus postal worker. Carol had worked in the mailroom for what was probably the better part of the twentieth century. She had shiny silver hair and piercing eyes and knew the names, birth dates, and probably Social Security numbers of every student on campus. I loved her.

"Mornin', Molly! Happy birthday! Look at you all fancy with this certified letter. Know who it's from?" she asked.

"Not a clue. But I'll let you know if it's from Publishers Clearing House!" I joked.

I signed for the letter, hugged Carol, and went off to see if anything else was in my mailbox. I grabbed a few birthday cards and a J.Crew catalog,[†] then went to sit down in the student lounge area and open up my birthday cards. One from my dad, one from my sister, and another one from my aunt.

The certified letter actually came in a large cardboard mailer. As I tore open the top, the dust from the cardboard got all over my black pants. I pulled out a thick stack of paperwork, and on top was a printed check. The physical size of the check was unusually small compared to the unusually large number written on it.

The check was made out to me, Molly Eileen Buckley, in the amount of $245,485.74.

The stack of paperwork fell into my lap, but I couldn't even read it in that moment. All I saw in my hands was a check for $245,485.74.

I didn't blink. My mouth was agape. I felt dizzy. My head was spinning. I sank farther into my seat, nervous that people walking by would see what I was holding. I looked to my left and right and was suddenly hyperaware of everyone and everything surrounding me. All of these people were just going about the day, living their lives, playing

---

† If only it had been a dELiA's catalog. Then I could have circled all the things I wanted with a Mr. Sketch marker!

pool in the student activity center, studying on nearby couches, buying books and Chick-fil-A, and *not* holding checks for $245,485.74.

And there I was, nonchalantly sitting on a couch in the middle of the student union next to a couple of pool tables, holding a check for $245,485.74. The seventy-four cents were just so . . . specific.

Not to mention that this check was made out to . . . *me*.

While I certainly didn't expect to receive the check at that very moment, the check didn't arrive *entirely* out of the blue. Let me back up for a second. For a few months, there had been some rumblings that I might (keyword: *might*) receive a small (keyword: *small*) inheritance—the amount of which, I had no idea. Not long before this, I'd been informed that my last living grandparent, my estranged grandmother (we will call her Noni)—my mom's mom—had died back in November 2004. Seeing as how I was estranged from that side of the family, no one had even bothered to tell me she had died. And, as a result of her death (and the fact that it was my twenty-first birthday), I found myself in possession of a check for $245,485.74.

"Um, how?" you ask. I understand you have questions. I'd love to answer them.

You see, many years ago, my maternal grandfather (we will call him Poppy) had purchased some properties in the heart of Georgetown, a real swanky area in Washington, DC. You've likely heard of it, as there is a very well-known university there that goes by the same moniker. It was my understanding that Poppy owned the properties for decades, renting them out to club owners, restaurants, and other bigwigs in the DC area. Poppy had set those properties up as a trust for his five children. When he passed away in 1996, the trust remained with Noni until her passing in 2004.

After Noni died, the executors of the will sold off each of the properties, and the proceeds from those sales were divvied up five ways—a portion for each of Noni and Poppy's five daughters. Since my mom had died, her share then went to me as her only direct descendant. (My older sister, Bridgid, is technically my half-sister, but we share the same dad.) However—*and here's the kicker*—the trust created by Poppy stated that if one of the Van Devanter children had passed away (as my mom had), the next eligible heir (me) would have to be *twenty-one years of age* before becoming eligible to receive their share of the inheritance.

Hence, this is how I found myself staring at a check for $245,485.74 on the morning of my twenty-first birthday.

Happy birthday to me.

Though I'd known an inheritance was a possibility, I was certainly unaware of the large amount. I also had good reason to believe this would never in a million years actually happen—mainly because my mother's family hated us and wanted nothing to do with me or my dad. I'd had zero relationships with any of them, including Noni, for nearly a decade by this point. I mean, no one had even told me that my grandmother had died. I assumed that any connection to my mom or our family had been written out of any remaining will or trust. Additionally, communication with them was entirely nonexistent, so everything I had heard was through the grapevine—and we all know how that goes. This is why an inheritance wasn't even remotely on my radar.

When I woke up that day, I certainly didn't have "inherit a quarter of a million dollars" on my twenty-first birthday bingo card.

I sat on the couch in that student lounge for what felt like an hour, staring protectively at that massive check. I had so many questions.

The first question was purely logistical: *So, um, what do I do with this? In a practical sense. Do I just, like, walk into a bank with this check and walk up to the teller and say, "Hi there. I'd like to deposit this check for $245,485.74"? You know, super casual. Regular Tuesday stuff.*

Then I wondered: *Do I cash this check and put all of the money in a briefcase like some James Bond character and hide it under my bed in my apartment? What if my RA finds it during quarterly inspections? Will the briefcase full of cash distract from the copious amount of candles and the cat named Harley I have in my apartment, both of which are definitely against the residential code of conduct?‡ Is being in possession of this check illegal too? Why does all of this feel illegal?*

I was spiraling.

So I did what any average twenty-one-year-old would do at this juncture. I stood up, gathered my wits and my belongings, put the check in my backpack, and walked to my 10:00 a.m. class.

Which I was already late for.

---

‡ What exactly is the statute of limitations for violating campus residence-hall policies?

2

BOY MEETS GIRL

FALL 1984

Worse than the ordinary miserable childhood
is the miserable Irish childhood, and worse yet
is the miserable Irish Catholic childhood.

FRANK MCCOURT

While, Lord willing, I've got a lot of life left to live, I've lived a lot of life up to now. In no way has it been a straight path; instead, it's been much more of a winding mountain road with a bunch of those "runaway truck" exits with the sand hills along the way. But only with the gift of hindsight can any of us say, "Oh, yeah, that tracks."

In my case, I can look back and see that the asphalt, rocks, dirt, and cobblestones on the life-path were being made and laid even decades before I was born.

It's a tale as old as time. Recovering alcoholic Irish Catholic girl meets recovering alcoholic Irish Catholic boy. They meet where all Irish Catholic recovering alcoholic folks meet: in an Alcoholics Anonymous (AA) meeting. They're both dating other people, but they quickly grow in their fondness for one another. Their relationships with their significant others end, and they find themselves single at the same time.

One evening, during a rousing game of Trivial Pursuit with mutual friends, boy and girl are on opposing teams. Boy reads the question that, if answered correctly by girl's team, will determine the winner of the game.

Boy reads, *"In August 1969, Upstate New York was home to a legendary music festival with nearly four hundred thousand people in attendance. Name them."*

Yes, our boy has made up the second part of the question. Our girl cackles in laughter. At that moment, girl is smitten with boy.

The problem: Boy and girl have only *very* recently ended serious relationships. It isn't the right time! Then again, when is the time ever right?

On Labor Day, boy is heading to Harpers Ferry for a picnic with his daughter from a previous marriage. (Oh yeah, I should mention that our Catholic boy is divorced . . . twice. Annnnnd, come to mention it, our Catholic girl is also divorced, but only once. Although she was engaged twice. So it's almost the same thing.) While getting a bag of ice at the local 7-Eleven, boy runs into girl.

"What are you up to?" the girl says.

"Heading out for a picnic with my daughter. Wanna come?" the boy asks.

"Sure!" the girl replies.

Boy and girl spend the day at Harpers Ferry with boy's daughter. They play in the river, eat a nice lunch, and enjoy the scenery. As they're walking back to the car at the end of the day, boy's nine-year-old daughter, Bridgid, is up ahead of them, skipping along the path. Girl is walking ahead of boy when suddenly boy stops. Girl turns around and looks at boy so earnestly and says, "You comin'? What's wrong?"

Boy replies, "You're going to think this is crazy. But it's just that you and I are going to get married, and we are going to have a baby girl named Molly."

Boy immediately thinks to himself, *Wait, what did I just say? Where in the world did that come from?*

Two weeks later, girl invites boy over for dinner. They laugh and talk and, strangely, they both know this is it. Boy knows he's going to propose.

The next week, boy buys a ring. While in the car together after picking up the ring, boy invites girl to get lunch with him at a local Jewish delicatessen. While waiting for their pastramis-on-rye and turkeys-on-wheat, boy gets down on one knee and asks girl to marry him. Everyone in the Jewish delicatessen is cheering, and girl says yes. On October 20, 1984, just shy of six weeks after their first date, boy, at the ripe age of forty, and girl, at the ripe age of thirty-seven, wed in holy matrimony. Ten months later (and a few weeks early), at eight pounds and some odd ounces, Molly Eileen Buckley is born.

This, believe it or not, is the story of how I came to be.

But how did our boy and our girl get there? What weird confluence of events led to their fateful meeting? Each of their stories, individually, could be a book of its own. (Come to think of it, my mom's was! You should read it! It's called *Home Before Morning*!) My dad could easily write eight books of random wild stories of his life without breaking a sweat, but he's too retired to do that, so I'll have to sum it up for you as best I can.

———

My dad, Charles Thomas "Tom" Buckley, *our aforementioned recovering alcoholic Irish Catholic boy*, was born in Cleveland, Ohio, on June 5,

1944. Yes, he was born the day before D-Day during World War II. His father, my Grandpa Charlie, a first lieutenant in the army, was stationed overseas at the time fighting with the Fifth Infantry throughout France and into Germany. Dad's mother, Erla, gave birth on her own, like many other women of that time, having no idea if her husband would ever make it home.

The first six years of Dad's life were spent in a four-hundred-square-foot apartment in the housing projects of downtown Cleveland. My dad was the oldest brother to four younger sisters—Margaret (Peggy), Patricia (Patty), Kathleen (Kathy), and Deborah (Debbie). *Ah, the names of the '40s and '50s.*

My dad had a tough relationship with his dad, Grandpa Charlie. He loved him, but there were never hugs or "I love yous," and Charlie never called my dad by his name. It was always "Herman," "Skinny," or "Lumpy." Only when he'd introduce my dad to someone would he refer to him as Tommy. Charlie was incredibly hardworking and always had a couple of jobs to support the family. But he was silent about his time in the war.

In the summer of 1950, thanks to the GI Bill, Charlie and Erla were able to move Dad and two of his baby sisters out of their apartment in the projects to an eight-hundred-square-foot home in the suburbs of Cleveland.

My dad describes his mother, Erla, as a beautiful, kind, loving mom with a sharp wit and a killer sense of humor. He always said his mom was the one he got his sense of humor from. Erla loved everyone and always did whatever she could to care for everyone else. She worked day and night keeping the home and five kids. Charlie adored Erla, and the two were deeply in love. Their different personalities, in many ways, balanced each other out, and they kept one another in line.

Dad, like all good Irish Catholic boys, spent his early years in

Catholic school. The nuns terrified him. In the first grade, he was so terrified of Sister Mary Padua that he refused to raise his hand and ask to go to the bathroom, so he peed himself right in his desk chair. His mom had to come pick him up early, and Sister Mary Padua lambasted him for it.

It was pretty much downhill from there. At the beginning of second grade, he and his buddy Bruce walked into the classroom to find their classmate Lois Hefferly dead on the floor, lying in a pool of her own urine. The boys stood there stunned, staring at their friend Lois. Their teacher, Sister Mary Ignatius, whisked Dad, Bruce, and the other classmates out into the hallway and told them to be quiet. They were held there until the situation with Lois was dealt with, but no one ever spoke of what happened. There was no class prayer for Lois; there was no Mass for Lois. To this day, no one has any idea as to what happened to Lois Hefferly.

Suffice it to say, that event scarred Dad; from that day forward, he was not about to step out of line when it came to the nuns. He thought becoming an altar boy would keep him in the good graces of the nuns and make him an extra good Catholic boy. By the eighth grade, Dad and his buddy Frankie Mishaga had risen through the ranks of the altar boys to *guardian* altar boys. Basically, it meant they got to do the "fun stuff" like weddings, funerals, and midnight masses. It also meant they got to leave class from time to time to serve Mass.

One particular day, Frankie and Dad got called out of class to serve a funeral. As they were cleaning up in the sacristy, a gentleman in the funeral party came to the back and handed Frankie and Dad each a ten-dollar bill. At the time, Dad had a morning route as a paperboy making two cents per paper. So ten dollars was like a million bucks to these boys. They were ecstatic!

A few moments later, Sister Mary Virginette (Dad said she must have been a tiny virgin) came into the sacristy to check on the boys' cleanup progress.

"Sister Mary Virginette! Guess what?!" Dad exclaimed. "This nice man from the funeral party gave us each ten dollars to thank us for serving today."

"How wonderful," said Sister Mary Virginette, as she proceeded to take the money from each of them.

The boys were stunned. A few moments later, she returned and handed each boy one dollar back. Then she walked out.

Dad and Frankie were livid.

"This is total hogwash!" Dad cried. "To heck with these people. To heck with all of this. You know what we're gonna do, Frankie? Come with me . . ." Dad's resentment toward the church had been building slowly since the incidents in the first and second grades, and by this point, Dad was done.

Dad led Frankie over to a special case that contained the monsignor's special Communion elements, which included an unopened bottle of special Italian wine just for the monsignor and a cookie tin filled with unblessed Communion hosts.

Dad popped open that bottle of wine, opened the cookie tin of hosts, and said, "Screw you, Sister Mary Virginette!" He poured two glasses for him and Frankie, and the two thirteen-year-old eighth graders proceeded to toast to Sister Mary Virginette, down the bottle, and eat all the hosts.

By the time they were supposed to head back to class, Dad and Frankie were drunk. Hammered. Toast. Gone. Blitzed. When the two stumbled back into class, their teacher, Sister Mary Georgine (who was at least 750 years old), sat at her desk, cane in hand, and yelled at the boys to "quiet down now!"

The next year, Dad went to public high school.

That incident was in large part what led Dad down a path of alco-holism. He found alcohol to be his primary tool against resentment for anything in life. In high school, his dad got him a job working downtown at the *Plain Dealer*, Cleveland's newspaper. At the end of the day, the older guys he worked with would take him next door to Headliner, a bar that never asked how old he was—and soon Dad learned how to smoke and put back a number of beers. At fourteen years old, he loved being one of the guys.

On June 5, 1962—the day he graduated from high school—he also turned eighteen, got his draft card, and wanted to enlist. Charlie, however, wouldn't allow him. "You're going to college," Charlie said.

That fall, Dad started at Bowling Green State University. His time at Bowling Green was pretty textbook (pun intended). He pledged a fraternity, got a degree, and landed a job as a high school English teacher in downtown Cleveland. After graduating, he reluctantly got married just weeks before his mom, Erla, died of breast cancer. His wife had so badly wanted to get married, and he only obliged because he felt like it was something he needed to do.

It didn't take long to realize he'd made a huge mistake. He worked all the time and drank all the time, and his new wife slept with her bosses all the time. They divorced six years later.

Dad maintained his job as a teacher, but his drinking got worse. A few years later, when he was president of the Cleveland teachers' union, he met Joann, the secretary. Not long after, they were married and had their daughter, Bridgid.

For a variety of reasons, Dad and Joann left teaching and moved to Dayton, Ohio, in 1974. There, Bridgid was born. Then in 1975, they left Ohio altogether and moved to Falls Church, Virginia.

Dad and Joann both drank heavily and fought constantly. When Bridgid was three, Joann kicked Dad out of the house with only a trash bag of his belongings, and for the next year, Dad was homeless. He slept in his rusty car, behind buildings, or on park benches.

On July 22, 1979, Dad called Joann to see if he could see Bridgid. He hadn't seen her in months. Joann said yes, so he drove from a motel room in Richmond to Arlington to pick her up. He took her with him to the American Legion club, where he could drink ten-cent beers and Bridgid could play pinball. The next morning, Dad woke up in a motel room in Richmond with his daughter lying next to him. He had no memory of making the hundred-mile drive and no idea how they'd gotten there.

He lay in the hotel room crying, then called out to God for help: "God, I can't do this anymore. I don't know what to do, but I need your help."

Dad opened his wallet and found a business card for a woman with ASAP, the Alcohol Substance Action Program. Her name was Normal Leeward. He had no idea where the card had come from, but when he showed up at her office, she said, "Oh my God, it's you!"

He'd never met her before in his life.

She took him to an AA meeting that day, and he was put in a twenty-one-day rehab program. At the time of this writing, he hasn't had a drink in more than forty-four years.

My dad has been and will always be one of the funniest, most hardworking people I know. He's never without a joke, a silly voice, a sarcastic remark, or a funny old-movie quote. He's happiest smoking a cigar and playing a round of golf. His life motto is: "Growing old is mandatory; growing up is optional." He also has been known to say that you can "never be sad when you're wearing purple."

My mom, Lynda Van Devanter, *our aforementioned recovering alco-holic Irish Catholic girl*, was born in Arlington, Virginia, on May 27, 1947. She and her four sisters were born to Helen and Rodney Van Devanter. She was raised your typical all-American girl of the '40s, '50s, and '60s. From going to church to playing baseball, camping with her family, watching TV, and performing in plays—everything about her childhood was what you'd expect from an average suburban middle-class family.

Helen made a full-time job of homemaking for my mom and her sisters. Rodney was a graduate of Georgetown University who worked for the civil service commission. Both of Mom's parents did all they could to emphasize the importance of duty to family, community, church, country, and all of mankind. Rodney especially did his best to instill in them a deep love and feeling for the Catholic faith.

During her childhood and early teenage years, my mom followed her father's example by attending Mass with him early on weekday mornings even when it wasn't required. When asked what she wanted to be when she grew up, she'd say "a martyr" because—according to her book, *Home Before Morning*—while "good Catholic boys usually fantasize about becoming major league baseball players or professional basketball stars, good Catholic girls usually harbor, at least once in their lives, a secret desire to become martyrs. If I couldn't make it to martyrdom, there was always sainthood."

She was incredibly close with her father, Rodney. Mom learned that before she was born, her parents had lost a son at birth. Then when Mom was born, she filled that "son role" for her father in many ways. She was a tomboy who loved playing sports with her dad in addition to performing in cabarets with him.

She grew up attending Catholic school until, as the legend goes, she was kicked out just before high school when a nun caught her smoking in the dressing room of a JCPenney. This is the only story I was ever told about why she was switched to public school, and it's the story I love to believe. I mean, picture this: My mother as a young teen in the late 1950s on a rebellious streak . . . she heads into her local James Cash Penney department store, lights one up in the dressing room, and who discovers her?! None other than Sister Mary Eunice. The whole mental image makes me laugh so much. Also, why did she have to smoke in a dressing room? What was a nun doing there? I have so many questions.

By the time she was twelve, Mom had given up her dreams of martyrdom and the *more realistic* dreams of becoming an actress and a singer. Mom was a natural caretaker, caring for just about everyone around her. She worked at a hospital as a volunteer and later as a nurse's aide. When her mother, Helen, got sick, my mom jumped right in to care for her through a long illness. So, naturally, Mom set her sights on a career in nursing. She saw nursing as her way of contributing to society. She idolized women like Florence Nightingale and Clara Barton and looked to them for inspiration.

After graduating from Yorktown High School in 1965, she went on to Mercy Hospital School of Nursing in Baltimore, Maryland. Though she had been raised in a Catholic home and had attended Catholic school, none of that prepared her for the rigors of nurses' training under the sisters of Mercy. Three long, hard years of classroom work, courses at Baltimore Junior College, prayer, and study barely left any time for shenanigans, as she liked to say. Except for one night when Mom and her friends decided to hold Mrs. Chase out of a third-floor window, begging her not to jump, much to the horror of the passersby below. Who was Mrs. Chase, you ask?

Well, the "Fundamentals of Nursing" classroom at Mercy held the infamous Chase family: Mr. Chase, Mrs. Chase, and Baby Chase—anatomically correct rubber dolls meant to serve as instructional tools. Needless to say, the Chase family was often used for more nefarious purposes.

But near the end of her time at Mercy, as you'll soon learn, life for Mom would change dramatically.

The Mom I knew was wildly talented. She had a beautiful singing voice, and she used to sing lullabies and "My Favorite Things" from *The Sound of Music* to me every night. She was a gifted writer, a dynamic speaker, and a *very* loud laugher. When you asked her for the time, she would build you a clock. She loved a fountain Diet Coke and was almost never without one in her thirty-two-ounce reusable jug. She wouldn't eat red meat because the smell reminded her of Vietnam. Her favorite cereal was All-Bran, and she'd "sweeten it up" by pouring a pack of raisins on top. She was incapable of leaving the house without it looking like she was moving out.

She was also selfless. If we passed by a person experiencing homelessness, she'd stop and offer to buy them lunch or hand them a gift card to McDonald's so they could get something to eat. She helped countless people through detox or rehab. She let anyone stay with us who needed a place to crash. She constantly thought of others before herself. I guess that's why her career path took her in the direction it did.

Mom never shied away from hard conversations and was willing to answer just about any question I had. The problem for me was, as a young kid, I often didn't know the questions I needed to ask . . . until it was too late.

By the time my parents met, they'd both lived a whole lot of life. They used to say they weren't each other's better half, but rather, together, they made a whole person. My parents weren't perfect, but they were perfect for each other.

Their unique upbringings and unique experiences in life made for a unique style of parenting and, ultimately, a unique childhood for me.

3

WHERE ARE THE CAMERAS?

1987–1994

When Molly was young, we knew she'd grow
up to either be president or go to jail.

MY DAD

Just as my dad so weirdly predicted on my parents' first date (if you can even call that outing a "date"), they got married and had a girl named Molly. In the most on-brand way possible, I came into this world keeping my parents on their toes. My mom had me at age thirty-eight, and while I wasn't due until the end of September, I made my entrance almost a month early and *still* weighed almost nine pounds. I was born with a heart murmur and a host of other random things that landed me a nice, comfy stay in the NICU for the first few weeks of my life.

My mom loved being a mom and wanted to do whatever possible to make sure she was doing things "right." There weren't parenting bloggers or moms on Instagram to show her the way, but there was Dr. T. Berry Brazelton and his complete set of Touchpoints VHS tapes. She loved that guy. She was also all about childhood enrichment, taking me to story time at the library and mommy-and-me exercise classes, or playing the concertos of Vivaldi or Chopin in my room because doing so would make me smarter.

It didn't take long for my personality to emerge, and it was a big one. I had colic, so I screamed constantly, and that didn't really stop once the colic went away. I had big feelings and wanted everyone in my general vicinity to know what those feelings were.

It was also the '80s, so my mom wouldn't let me chew gum but *would* let me drink Diet Coke. There's actual video evidence of my mom handing me a *glass bottle* full of Diet Coke on my second birthday, and me proceeding to chug the entire thing. *I come by my Diet Coke addiction honestly. Save your emails.*

As early as I could walk and talk, I was performing *something*. I'd dance, sing, and make stuff up for my parents and anyone else willing to humor me for even a moment. The summer I turned three, I was sitting at the kitchen table, unusually silent. I looked around, examining every nook and cranny of our kitchen. My brows furrowed, my lips pursed.

"What are you looking at?" Mom asked.

I took a beat and said, "Where are the cameras?"

"The cameras?" Dad asked.

"The cameras! Where are the cameras? For the show we are on?" I replied insistently.

Basically, in my three-year-old mind, I was convinced I was living in some version of *The Truman Show* long before *The Truman Show* actually existed.

My mom loved to psychoanalyze that moment, suggesting it was when I realized I was part of a bigger world and should find my place in society. I don't think it was all that serious; I just thought I was on a TV show.

When I was three, my parents put me in a half-day preschool program at the local high school. The high school had an early childhood development class and thought it would be a great idea for those students to work with really tiny people in the stages of early childhood.

On my first day of school, I woke up ready. I was *born* ready. I was going through a bit of a Judy Garland phase, so I dressed myself in my Dorothy from *The Wizard of Oz* costume because that was the only thing I would wear at the time. The costume included patent leather ruby-red slippers, a blue gingham dress, a braided wig, and a basket with a stuffed Toto. I was method acting. I also insisted on taking a lunchbox to school. So, after getting dressed, I grabbed my plastic Fisher-Price *Sesame Street* lunchbox, walked downstairs, and told my parents I was ready for the day. Rise and grind. I was into hustle culture before that was a thing.

Now, there was no lunch at school because it was only a half day. We didn't even need to bring a snack. So the lunchbox was completely empty. My parents decided this was not a battle worth fighting with me, so they got me in the car (since it was the '80s, I was probably not even buckled) and took me to school.

Mom and Dad walked me in, and I vividly remember the speckled linoleum floor and the red lockers lining the hallway. I also remember the big black-and-red hornet painted on the cinder block walls that said "Go Hornets!" underneath. We walked into the classroom and were greeted by my teacher, Mrs. Henning.

She smiled, bent over, and said, "Oh, hello! You must be Molly!"

To which I replied, "NO!" I screamed it at the top of my lungs and proceeded to smack Mrs. Henning upside the head with my empty *Sesame Street* lunchbox. I assaulted my teacher on the first day. Great start!

It didn't get much better from there. When my fellow classmates were playing a game I didn't want to play, I would sit on the game. If anyone referred to me by a name *other* than Dorothy (because *that was who I was*—could they not see I was method acting?!), I would push them and run away. Lord, bless my poor parents.

I did get better and eventually straightened out, and by the time I graduated from preschool right before I turned five, Mrs. Henning had really grown to love me after two years of her tutelage. Somehow I'd endeared myself to the rest of the early childhood education students too.

———

By the time I got to elementary school, I was a little less like a ticking time bomb and more like a nuclear power plant: I generated a ton of energy, and you really didn't want me to explode. I was an awkward kid in so many ways. I know every parent says their kid is cute, and maybe I was, but the fact that I hadn't lost my baby cheeks *and* had a mullet—a real-life, actual mullet—did not help my case.

I laughed *all the time* and very loudly, and I wanted everyone else to laugh too. I wanted that so badly that I ended up peeing my pants a few times because I was so focused on entertaining others or laughing at myself that I wouldn't go to the bathroom until it was too late. Then I'd laugh again and pee myself *more*.

This was particularly unfortunate on one occasion when my mom had dressed me in an all-white sweat suit from Kmart. She'd even ironed on Christmas wreath appliqués and embellished them with red-and-green glitter puffy paint around the edges. My first-grade class was headed to a holiday assembly, I was cutting up as per usual, and I peed myself all down my white Kmart sweat suit. Mom was away on business at the time, and since Dad was at work, no one was able to bring a new set of clothes to school. I had to walk around *the rest of the day* in my pee-covered sweat separates. I loved it. It was great. Highly recommend. I've absolutely gotten over it by this point in life.

I eventually adjusted, but not without a lot of work.

I also wanted to be just like my mom. As you'll hear more about in the next chapter, my mom was a fierce advocate and fighter for veterans—women veterans more specifically. But her dedication to her advocacy meant I would travel with her to her speaking engagements. I met congressmen and congresswomen, I met Colin Powell, and I even attended congressional hearings. These experiences taught me how to lobby for late bedtimes, dessert before dinner, and more Saturday morning cartoons!

But they also had healthy and constructive effects too.

This manifested itself in a big way in March 1994. After school, I'd do what most other kids my age would do: go outside and play for hours on end. I was one of the older kids in my neighborhood, so I took it upon myself to be somewhat of a guardian for all the little ruffians. We lived in the historic part of our town, which meant there were no sidewalks to be found. On multiple occasions, I'd watch cars ignore the twenty-five mph speed limit signs, whoosh down our road, and nearly hit children playing in the street.

On one particularly harrowing occasion, my best friend Phong was almost hit by a car. I immediately ran inside to tell my parents. "*Mom. Dad.* We need sidewalks. How do we get sidewalks?"

My parents said, "Well, you go to the town council meeting and tell them we need sidewalks."

What?! That's it? Simple as that? Sweet.

So I did what any other normal eight-year-old would do: I went to look at the Town of Herndon calendar hanging in our foyer. As it turned out, a town council meeting was scheduled for *that night* at

7:00 p.m. . . . *Huzzah!* I went upstairs, turned on the family Macintosh Classic II, and I typed up a speech.*

Then I put on my green velvet dress that matched Samantha, my American Girl doll, and marched downstairs to inform my parents they would be driving me to the town council meeting that night.

My parents looked at each other like I was insane and said, "Okay."

They drove me downtown to the town hall and walked me into the large room where the mayor and town council sat. As soon as the mayor called for "any new citizen business," I marched myself up to the podium, pulled down that rickety Bob Barker–style microphone, and gave my speech demanding sidewalks for our neighborhood to keep the kids safe.

The speech (verbatim) read:

Mr. Mayor and Members of the Council.

My name is Molly Buckley. I live at _____ Jackson St. in Herndon, VA. I am 8 and a half years old.

I am here because our neighborhood needs some sidewalkes. I am the oldest kid in the neighborhood and there are lots of kids too. I've had to watch the kids play in the street because there parents are busy.

I have had to learn to be carefull playing in the street because there are no sidewalks. I had to learn how to ride my bike, roller skate, hopscotch, jump rope, and play other games.

It is scary watching the kids play in the street with cars coming. And it was scary for me learning how to play in the street with cars coming. We keep being told that we will get sidewalks, but we never do.

My request is for some sidewalks. Will you please give us some.

THANK YOU!†

---

* "Clippy," the little Microsoft Word paper clip guy, popped up and said, "It looks like you're writing a speech for a town council meeting! Can I help you with that?"

† It should be noted that the "thank you" was typed out in mid-1990s bold, outlined, purple typeface! Unfortunately, there was no clip art on the speech.

The mayor and the town council thought I was adorable, so they patronized me and said they'd "look into it." The story got big news coverage. I was on the cover of the *Herndon Times* and the *Herndon Observer*. "Eight-Year-Old Lobbies Town Council for Sidewalks." It was big-time stuff.

Three months went by; still no sidewalks. So I went *back* to the town council and delivered yet another speech. The mayor told me they'd "look into it" again.

Three more months later, no sidewalks. Clearly, my speeches were not working, so I started to write letters to the mayor. And when letters didn't work, I started to pick up the phone and call the mayor. When the calling didn't work, I started a petition, got signatures from my neighbors, and hand-delivered it to the mayor's office.

And then, after two and a half years of speeches, letters, petitions, and phone calls—two and a half years after my initial appearance before the town council—we got a knock on the door. It was a town council member along with a surveyor and an engineer, asking for Molly Buckley to come show them where to put the sidewalks.

And you can bet I wrote my name in the cement.

FOR MOLLY

What did you do in the war, Mommy?
Hazel eyes shining brightly
Pony tails bobbing softly
One pierced earring and an orange juice mustache.
Where did that man's arm go, Mommy?
Plastic slinky bouncing wildly
Tie dye T-shirt hanging loosely
Looks at me so earnestly I have to touch her.
I wrote a story about a war, Mommy.
Where nobody got guns or dead
This one was a good war
Don't you know?
Why do you have tears now, Mommy?
Little girl with dreams so peaceful
Alphabets and clowns and people
I don't want you growing up too soon.

—LYNDA VAN DEVANTER BUCKLEY,
VISIONS OF WAR, DREAMS OF PEACE

4

WHAT DID YOU DO IN THE WAR, MOMMY?

1960s–1990s

War is bad.

LYNDA VAN DEVANTER BUCKLEY

Those three words, cross-stitched in red thread on a white background, hung on the wall in my mom's office.

"Why is war bad, Mommy?" I asked. I was five, and while it was no secret to me that my mom had served in Vietnam, I had no clue what that *really* meant.

"Someday I'll tell you, sweetheart," she replied as she scooped me up in her arms. A tear ran down her cheek as she inhaled the smell of my hair. She kissed me on the temple and said, "I love you."

"I love you, too, Mommy."

The reality of what my mom did in the war in Vietnam would not be a sit-down, detailed conversation we would ever get to have. Rather, her story, her experience, and the war's aftermath became something I couldn't *not* learn, whether by simple osmosis or by sheer immersion in the last seventeen years of her life for the first seventeen years of mine.

———

Here's what Mommy did in the war.

During his inaugural address on January 20, 1961, President John F. Kennedy announced, "We shall pay any price, bear any burden, meet any hardship, support any friend, oppose any foe to assure the survival and the success of liberty." He would go on to conclude his address with his most iconic line: "And so, my fellow Americans: ask not what your country can do for you—ask what you can do for your country." These words were taken to heart by many Americans at the time, but there was something about those words that sank deep into the recesses of my mom's heart. Kennedy's words shaped much of what Mom did, and ultimately, she made the biggest and most transformative decision of her life because of her belief in the sentiments expressed by that charismatic young president.

The first few years my mom was in nursing school, she hadn't paid much attention to the war in Vietnam. In school growing up, she'd barely even learned about the small Southeast Asian country. But during her time at Mercy, the news coverage about the war had only increased. It didn't take long before printed papers and television were bringing the daily news of the Vietnam War into homes, classrooms, restaurant conversations, and street corner talks. The war was everywhere.

During her senior year at Mercy, an army recruiter came to speak to the nursing students about serving in the war. Mom was one of the first in her group to stand up and say she would enlist. The decision, for her, was mostly an emotional one. She felt a strong desire to help those wounded American boys and knew that as a nurse she could serve her country well. "If those boys were being blown apart, then I needed to be the one over there putting them back together," she'd said. She also wanted to be "Florence Nightingale in green." While they feared for her safety, her parents were proud of her—especially her father.

Mom's graduation from nursing school at Mercy in 1968 was immediately followed by a wild road trip. Mom and her friend and fellow Mercy graduate Barbara took off in a 1962 Chevy Nova to drive across the country. Then Mom was sworn into the army on October 31, 1968, and she entered basic training at Fort Sam Houston in San Antonio, Texas. During basic training, they were taught how to march and how to polish the brass on their shoes by spitting on them. They learned how to (and whom to) salute and lots of other stuff that had absolutely *nothing* to do with their mission of saving lives. They also learned how to fire rifles and pistols, avoid booby traps, read a compass and a map, recognize the enemy, and do the iconic "low army crawl." All the while, she was being assured that as a nurse she would *never* be sent into combat zones.

Mom and Barbara took the medical portion of their training very seriously. They learned how to set up a field hospital, how to handle mass casualty situations, how to do triage, and how to perform emergency tracheostomies. After their basic training in San Antonio, Mom was sent to El Paso, Texas, for more extensive training in operating room nursing.

In June 1969, her orders for Vietnam finally arrived. Twenty-four hours later, she was on a plane.

During the early hours of the morning of June 8, 1969, twenty-five-year-old First Lieutenant Sharon A. Lane of Canton, Ohio, became the first army nurse to be killed in Vietnam as a result of hostile fire.

A Viet Cong rocket exploded next to the hospital hut in which she was working. A few hours later, my mom's plane landed in Vietnam.

It didn't take long for Mom to learn that no one, not even a nurse, was safe in Vietnam. Her first assignment was at the 71st Evacuation (Evac) Hospital in the mountains of Pleiku near the Cambodian border. This MASH-type hospital was situated in an area of heavy combat and seemingly unending casualties. Her first reaction at the mere sight of the 71st was total shock. The hospital was made up of ramshackle wooden buildings and metal huts. A layer of red dust and mud covered everything. The entire compound was surrounded by a high fence and barbed wire, all guarded by armed men in tanks.

The helicopter pad sat about fifty yards from the ER, which was directly connected to the operating room and intensive care units. The consternation she felt at seeing her new hospital would be nothing compared to what she felt when she reported for her first shift in the OR. By 71st standards, her first day was a slow one. *Only* fifteen wounded soldiers needed surgery. Their wounds were horrendous, ranging from ordinary gunshot wounds to amputations, to open gut wounds, to wounds caused by thousands of metal fragments being sprayed into the air, to horrific burns from napalm, to lower body injuries caused by the Bouncing Betty—a land mine that, when triggered, bounced up to waist level before exploding.

The nurses were scheduled to work twelve-hour shifts, but in reality, Mom and her colleagues often found themselves working for twenty-four-hour-plus stretches during periods of heavy fighting. Sleep was regularly interrupted by the booms of rocket attacks and whir of landing helicopters. More often than not, Mom would sleep under her bed to serve as protection from the rockets falling nearby. She would be so exhausted, she'd sometimes not even wake to the sound of the explosions. At times they almost became like white noise.

But as the saying goes: work hard, play hard.

Mom and her friends, when they weren't working, would do whatever they could to block out the horrors of what they were seeing day in, day out. Loud parties with lots of drinking, drugs, and loud music . . . men and women in both emotional and sexual relationships with one another despite having a husband or wife back home . . . It wasn't long before Mom found herself in an intimate relationship—both physically and emotionally—with Carl, an OR doctor who had a wife and kids back home.

One moment they'd be partying and dancing; the next moment they'd be coming under a rocket attack and soon operating on the incoming wounded. It wasn't uncommon for doctors or nurses to find themselves under the influence of something while caring for a patient. They would self-medicate with just about anything, if even for a moment, to escape their nightmare. It wasn't that they were drinking while on duty; they just wound up being on duty twenty-four hours a day, seven days a week.

War makes people do crazy things.

War is bad.

Throughout all of it, Mom tried hard to keep in close contact with her family by sending home letters and tapes. Her dad was proud of her for serving her country, while her mom just wanted her to come home alive. In all the letters and tapes Rodney and Helen sent back to my mom, they never mentioned the political turmoil and strife going on in America. But Mom could tell something was wrong.

"Please tell me you're flying the flag, Mom and Dad," she wrote. "We need to know our families back home believe in us and what we're doing over here. Please don't stop flying the flag."

"We're flying the flag," Rodney replied. "We're so very proud of you."

As the months in Vietnam passed, she became more and more disillusioned and angry. She was angry at the government for sending troops to Vietnam. She was angry with all the death. She was angry with all the destruction. She was angry with all the disease. She was angry at God. She was angry with Vietnam itself. She was still proud to be an American, but while she knew she was the difference between life and death for the soldiers she cared for, she also felt it was all so very senseless.

She started having nightmares, seeing the faces and mangled bodies of the dead and dying soldiers she cared for in her dreams. Before long "Vietnam sucks" became their mantra and belief.

The turning point for her was on her "Hump Day"—the halfway mark of her tour in Vietnam. Amid a particularly brutal mass casualty (mass-cal) situation, everyone was running around frantically caring for the injured and dying. Patients were triaged and categorized as "expectant" or "viable." Expectant meant there was nothing that could be done and the patient was expected to die. Viable meant they had a chance.

It was hectic.

One patient had come onto her table, blown to bits and loosely held together by bone and sinew. His face had been mostly blown off, his lungs were collapsed, and blood was everywhere. She did everything she could to focus on the task at hand, but there was something about this boy she couldn't shake. He was expectant, yes. This young boy, this soldier, was going to die. He wasn't the first young boy she'd seen die, but something about him was different.

At some point, she'd kicked the clothes that had been cut off his body to the side. Then a picture fell out of the front pocket of his fatigues. A snapshot. She lifted it up and held it in her hands as her eyes fell on the young couple in the photo. It was a prom photo: the boy dressed in a tuxedo and cummerbund, and the young girl in a beautiful dress with a corsage. On the back of the picture was written "Gene and Katie, May 1968."

Gene and Katie.

May 1968.

He was real. He was Gene. She was Katie. Together they were Gene and Katie. He was just a kid who had been to the prom the year before. Gene loved Katie. Katie loved Gene. Gene was going to die. All Mom could do in that moment was think about the uniformed officer who would show up at Gene's house to tell his parents. All she could do was picture Katie getting a phone call.

Mom was angry. She was devastated. She was destroyed. She was changed.

That was the moment she knew the Lynda she was before the war was gone forever.

War is bad.

———

Eventually Mom was moved from the 71st to the 67th Evacuation Hospital in Quy Nhon, a city on the coast. There she would spend her last few weeks in Vietnam. This hospital wasn't located in a combat zone, and the pace and stress were much less severe than at the 71st. The staff mostly worked regular twelve-hour shifts and lived in real two-story buildings. They'd spend their free time going to the beach, going on picnics, or even working with local Vietnamese civilians.

Weekly, Mom would go with the eye surgeon from the 67th Evac to a local leper colony run by an order of French nuns. (No, this is not the setup of a joke.) They'd do everything from providing routine medical care to performing necessary, lifesaving surgeries. She really enjoyed her work with the lepers because the patients were grateful and the colony itself was situated in a beautiful valley. This was a much-needed change from the heat of the DMZ (demilitarized zone) and her usual routines and mass-cals.

But as the final months of her tour dragged on, going home consumed her thoughts. She'd mark off each day on her calendar as a countdown to when she'd get on that "Freedom Bird" and be back on US soil. She continued to send and receive letters and tapes from her dad. She included the following message in her book *Home Before Morning*:

> Hi, Lynda, this is Dad. My little girl's coming home soon. I
> can't wait. I don't guess we'll be sending too many more
> of these tapes back and forth, so I won't be running at the
> mouth much longer. I can't wait until you get home. We all
> miss you very much. This is your loving daddy signing off.
> Good night, Lynda.

She was allowed a brief "vacation" near the end of her tour, so she and her friend Mickie decided on Thailand since it was exotic, tropical, and easy to get to from Vietnam. They spent most of their time shopping, drinking, and eating. Mom was especially excited about her "souvenir" set of hand-carved bronze flatware, a set that was eventually passed down to me. (I still have it but am too afraid to actually use it for some reason.)

On June 16, 1970, a little over a year after she arrived, Mom returned home from Vietnam as a first lieutenant in the army—but she also returned a very different woman to a very different Divided States of America. She was not welcomed by a gaggle of people holding flags or "Welcome home!" signs. She was not greeted with hugs and flowers. She was not greeted by the general American public eager to show respect and thanks for her sacrifice and service. She wasn't greeted with a brass band or a parade. She wasn't even greeted with basic transportation from Travis Air Force Base to San Francisco International Airport twenty miles away so she could hop on a connecting flight to get home to her family. "I gave the army a year of my life," she said. "The least they could have given me was a ride."

She tried commercial buses and taxis, but none were running because of a transit strike going on. So she huffed her duffel on her shoulder, grabbed her suitcase and her purse, stood on the side of the road, stuck her thumb out, and waited.

This wasn't her first time hitchhiking. It was a common mode of transportation in Vietnam, but it was certainly her first time hitchhiking while wearing army fatigues and carrying a load of luggage in America. Cars would fly past her as she hoped, prayed, and waited for someone, *anyone*, to stop. Cars would slow down just to roll down their windows and give her the middle finger. Some yelled obscenities. One car threw a bag of trash at her, while another threw a half-empty can of soda.

"Welcome home, a**hole!" they yelled.

But then, a glimmer of hope. A red-and-yellow Volkswagen bus with two guys in it pulled over and slid open the side door. She ran right to the bus, dragging her duffel bag and luggage.

"Going anywhere near the airport?" she asked.

"Sure am," one guy said.

She breathed a sigh of relief and smiled. As she went to throw her luggage in the back of the van, he slammed the door shut in her face and yelled, "We're going past the airport, sucker, but we don't take army pigs." Then he inhaled and hocked a loogie on her.

"F*** you, Nazi b****," the driver yelled as they laughed, cackled, and sped away. Hours went by. She was so confused and hurt.*

No, upon her return from Vietnam, my mom wasn't greeted with pomp and circumstance. Instead, she was greeted with bitterness, anger, and indifference from a culture of people deeply divided over the controversy of the war.

———

Approximately ten thousand military women served in Vietnam, most of them nurses. These women were the youngest and least experienced group of healthcare workers ever to serve in wartime. They dealt with extraordinary injuries inflicted by weapons developed purely for the intention of mutilation and maiming. Over fifty-eight thousand soldiers died in Vietnam. Three hundred fifty thousand were wounded. "Somewhere between 1945 and 1970, words like bravery, sacrifice, and valor had gone out of vogue," my mom wrote. "When I returned to my country in June of 1970, I began to learn a very bitter lesson . . . In the eyes of most Americans, the military services had no more heroes, merely baby killers, misfits, and fools."

While her family received her somewhat warmly, they could not even begin to understand the changes they saw in her.

Then, the nightmares came. Mom described them as bloody parades of young men without arms or legs, with faces blown off, and with gaping abdominal wounds. Her drinking, a way to numb a fraction of the pain, got worse. She isolated herself from her friends

---

* The barrage of vulgar language hurled at Mom and other Vietnam veterans, in addition to the horrific treatment they received, was shocking not only to Mom at the time, but it still shocks me to this day. It is a painful reality in our history, and I'm grateful that our military service-women and servicemen are treated with the dignity, honor, and respect they deserve today.

and family and found it nearly impossible to form a lasting or stable relationship, despite feeling an overwhelming need for love and affection. She began to suffer from severe bouts of depression, crying for days at a time. She was unable to eat or sleep. She'd stay in bed all day. Her love of nursing had faded, and she found herself constantly changing jobs.

In the summer of 1971, she began to work as a dialysis nurse, doing in-home dialysis for kidney patients. She was fired the next January because of her frequency of missing work. It wasn't long before she ended up on unemployment and on food stamps.

She thought a lot about suicide. She drank herself into oblivion.

Eventually, she began to see a therapist. She'd spend long sessions talking about everything. Everything *but* Vietnam. In part, this was because when she tried to tell someone about her service, they often would say, "What do you mean you were in Vietnam? Women weren't in Vietnam, honey. Women don't go to war. Women can't be veterans."

It was hard enough being a Vietnam veteran, but being a woman Vietnam veteran was an added challenge she hadn't anticipated. She showed up to the Veterans Affairs office (VA) only to be turned away because "Women weren't in 'Nam." She was told she couldn't march with the Vietnam Veterans Against the War (VVAW) because she "didn't look like one." The public discussions in the early '70s addressed the need to "bring our boys home from Vietnam." Everywhere she went, people and politicians spoke of the needs of the "men" who fought the noble cause. There wasn't a single support program in place for women veterans.

All of this only further reinforced the suppression of her memories and experiences. So, even with the help of a professional, she couldn't bring herself to talk about what she'd experienced. She had buried the horrors of Vietnam so deeply.

Around that same time, she began dating Bill Blackton, a reporter she'd met through her dialysis work. He was the son of the Oscar-winning composer Jay Blackton, but Bill was an incredible and unique man in his own right—an award-winning journalist and one of the longest-living dialysis patients in the world. They married at Christmastime of 1975. However, those first few years of their marriage were incredibly challenging. Bill didn't know how to help Mom with all she was dealing with, including her flashbacks and nightmares. Mom had severe post-traumatic stress disorder (PTSD), but at the time, people didn't really have the resources or knowledge to name it.

In May 1979, while Mom and Bill were visiting friends on Long Island, New York, she was awoken in the middle of the night by a siren from a nearby firehouse. She instantly got up and army-crawled out of the house, just like she'd been trained. Bill eventually found her outside under a tree with her hands cupped over her head. He picked her up, wiped the tears from her face, held her in his arms, and whispered, "You're all right, Lynda. You're okay." But the thing was, she wasn't all right, nor was she okay.

They were in New York at the time because Bill happened to be doing a radio documentary on a newly formed organization called Vietnam Veterans of America (VVA). Mom met two of the group's directors, and as they started talking about their own experiences and the experiences of other Vietnam veterans, Mom didn't feel so alone for the first time in a long time. The next month, Mom was asked to form the Vietnam Veterans of America Women's Project (VVAWP).

She said yes, but on one condition: She needed a year to work on her marriage and get education and training that would enable her to help the women she'd be working with. When she and Bill returned to California, they started marriage counseling, and Mom signed up for psychology classes at Antioch University in Los Angeles to study the "plight of the Vietnam veteran." She went on to graduate with her bachelor's degree in psychology.

It was at this time she started learning about PTSD, which was rampant among veterans. Not only did Mom herself have nearly every sign and symptom of PTSD, but so did most of the other vets she interacted with.

Immersing herself in the preparation and planning for the VVAWP was just one step in the real healing journey for Mom. This work gave her renewed meaning, purpose, and drive.

In the summer of 1980, she made her first formal presentation on behalf of the VVAWP. During that time, she met a man by the name of Shad Meshad, a counselor who worked with Vietnam veterans. Shad helped her realize that for her to really make a difference in helping others, she had to finally come to terms with her own demons from Vietnam. She started doing intensive therapy with Shad. Her thoughts, feelings, and experiences became clearer, and she felt like she was exorcising a ghost she'd carried with her for over a decade.

While Shad helped Mom in countless ways, one of the most transformative moments was when she told Shad how unappreciated she'd felt. From how she was treated upon returning home to her dialysis work to her marriage to those she was trying to help—lack of appreciation underlined them all. Shad had been a psych officer in Vietnam and had known hundreds of nurses like Mom. He told her of the enormous respect he had for those nurses and how much of a difference they were making. While the jobs of nurses were incredibly overwhelming, he watched nurses triumph. And, most importantly, the nurses in Vietnam had saved the lives of thousands of men, women, and children who might have otherwise died.

"*You* [the women] were my heroes," Shad told her.

Hearing those simple words made Mom begin to believe in herself again.

Mom began to devote nearly every waking moment of her life to the cause of women veterans in Vietnam. She was constantly fighting stereotypes of what it looked like—and *didn't* look like—to serve in Vietnam. "Was it just like the television show *M*A*S*H*?" people would ask. To which she'd have to stop herself from punching them in the face.

Even though she and Bill worked hard to save their marriage, they realized they never should have married in the first place. In 1981, she and Bill divorced amicably and remained friends until Bill died in November 2000. I can attest to their friendship as I grew up; I knew Bill and his sister, Jennie, well and saw them regularly. Their relationship was as unique as they were. Mom cared deeply for the Blacktons and we were all devastated when Bill passed.

———

In 1982, Mom returned to Vietnam. Only this time, it was as a member of the VVA delegation working with the Vietnamese government on the issues of MIAs, POWs, Agent Orange, and Amerasian children. Returning to Vietnam had a profound impact on her healing journey, and on the plane home, she knew she had to tell her story, the whole story, to the world.

Writing was in Mom's blood. She kept extensive personal journals, wrote long letters, and had countless steno pads, notepads, and sticky pads scribbled with her thoughts. She wrote down just about everything. In the years after Vietnam, writing became a deeper, more personal form of therapy for her. She believed in the therapy of writing.

Soon her writings would also serve as therapy for others. And in the future, her writing would become therapy for me.

In 1983, Mom wrote and published her memoir, *Home Before Morning: The Story of an Army Nurse in Vietnam*. Her book was the first nonfiction account of the war from a woman's perspective. In more ways than one, it was groundbreaking. At the time, few were talking about the brutality of Vietnam, let alone the circumstances of women veterans.

Home Before Morning was her most personal, healing work, but the writing and publication of it became more divisive than she ever could have imagined. Her motives, her ethics, her values, her training, her courage, and her objectivity were praised by some, challenged by many, and called into question by others.

Those who had served in Vietnam fell into two groups. The first group included those who felt *Home Before Morning* finally gave voice to the harsh realities of war. The raw, honest storytelling was healing for them. Mom held nothing back in her book. She wanted to paint a realistic picture of what the war was like, not what many came to think it was from the show *M*A*S*H* (even though *M*A*S*H* was set during the Korean War). Many finally felt seen by the words written in *Home Before Morning*.

War is bad, after all.

The other group, on the other hand, felt differently. A civilian nurse named Pat Walsh led the charge, and in 1985, she formed a group called NAM (Nurses Against Misrepresentation). This group of nurses claimed that the accounts recorded in *Home Before Morning* were more fiction than fact, that Mom was telling a sensationalized story, and ultimately that they were concerned the families of those men and women who had died in Vietnam would question whether or not they'd received the best care if their doctors and nurses were potentially under the influence.

However, there may have been a more sinister, ulterior motive. In the years after its release, *Home Before Morning* had grown in popularity and gained a lot of traction. In 1985, Mom was approached by actress Sally Field, and Columbia Pictures had spoken to Mom about making the book into a movie.[†] When Field made the announcement of the option, Walsh, who had released a fictional account of the war in 1982, came out of the woodwork and began the smear campaign.

It got ugly. Fast.

The experience nearly bankrupted my parents. They'd married in October 1984, and I was born the following August. In that span of time, they were thrust into legal battles and heated debates.

Mom found herself defending her story on national nightly news programs from *Larry King Live* to *60 Minutes*. She was interviewed and challenged in every major publication from the *New York Times* to *Time* to the *San Francisco Chronicle*. The controversy was thick. It eventually got so bad and so divisive that Sally Field pulled out of the option to make the movie.

Nurses would contact Mom and privately tell her they supported her, believed her, identified with her story, and knew what she said was true. However, they were too afraid to support her publicly for fear of what their support might do to *them*.

Mom would be invited to events for veterans, only to be uninvited in the hallway as she was walking in for fear of "the controversy" her presence would bring.

This abandonment from so many devastated her. However, she had friends, groups, and supporters who *didn't* abandon her, who came

---

† While the movie was never made, the late 1980s CBS show *China Beach* starring Dana Delany was made and used *Home Before Morning* as the inspiration for the story. However, because of the controversies around Mom's book, *China Beach* changed *just enough* that they never had to pay her a dime for her work. Nor did they officially credit her for it. That said, it is widely accepted as the inspiration behind the show.

to her defense regardless. She clung to and cultivated those relationships like her life depended on it.

I had a front-row seat to watching my mom heal. I saw her fight against all odds for what she knew was right. I saw her stand up in the face of incredible adversity and pave a path for those who were right behind her. It was not easy, but it was important, and she knew that.

I saw the tears and the pain in her eyes turn to joy, laughter, and peace. I clapped and cheered along with her as I watched her stand beside General Colin Powell, Senator John Kerry, and fellow army nurse and founder of the Vietnam Veterans Women's Memorial Project, Diane Carlson Evans, as they held shovels at the groundbreaking of the Vietnam Women's Memorial in Washington, DC. A truly momentous occasion.

By the early 1990s, Mom had reached a place where she not only felt proud to be a veteran but also felt whole again. It had taken years of personal work, intense counseling, prayer, and healing for Mom to get to a place where the war, or other people's words, no longer had full control of her life.

But it's never that simple, is it? Because war always finds a way. The war would soon take control of the rest of her life in a much different way.

5

DEAD BIRDS IN THE WALLS

FALL 1994

I am ready to face any challenges that
might be foolish enough to face me.

DWIGHT SCHRUTE

I lived in the same house from birth until I went to college. It was an old tin-roofed, turn-of-the-century farmhouse situated in the heart of downtown Herndon, Virginia. The house was built in 1900, and my mom bought it, by herself, in the late summer of 1981. (From here on out, I'm gonna refer to the house as the Jackson Street house because that's what it'll always be to me.)

At the time Mom bought the Jackson Street house, it had no HVAC system, only one electrical outlet downstairs, one electrical outlet upstairs (both of which had extension cords running from them), one bathroom, a barely usable kitchen, and a whole lot of holes in the walls. But! In the living room, it had a brick fireplace with an antique wooden mantel and mirror above it, and a bay window she knew would be perfect for a Christmas tree . . . So she bought it. Yes, she bought a house entirely because of the potential Yuletide joy it would bring.

Jackson Street was the very epitome of a fixer-upper. In order to even complete the purchase, my mom had to put in an HVAC unit, route ductwork throughout the house, add more outlets, and remove the extension cords strewn about the house because—hello!—fire hazard. The house wasn't even up to 1980s code, which at the time was essentially "Is the house *currently* on fire? Nope? Great, you're all set! Welcome home!"

My mom liked to joke that the only reason she married my dad was because he knew how to install drywall, which the home needed a lot of.

Jackson Street also had a dungeon-looking basement with stone walls, which flooded every time the weather thought about raining. It also had a walk-up attic that was eleventy billion degrees in the summer and an arctic tundra in the winter. (The attic was eventually "finished," as in "drywalled" [Go, Dad!]. After carpet was added, the attic became my bedroom in high school.)

While Jackson Street went through many iterations of paint colors during my childhood and teen years, I remember it best with its baby-blue wooden siding and bubble-gum pink trim. This color palette was apparently due to a mix-up with the paint order, but my mom liked the finished product too much to fix it. The colors made Jackson Street look like a real, honest-to-goodness dollhouse.

The front porch had a swing and old, wooden lattice that lined its base. On every Mother's Day, my dad would get large baskets of impatiens to hang between every beam of the porch. He'd lovingly care for those impatiens all summer until the baskets were bursting at the seams with flowers. The creaky old screen door covering the front door sounded like Auntie Em's house in *The Wizard of Oz* when you opened it and it immediately slammed shut. Inside the foyer was an antique Tiffany-style Victorian chandelier and the most beautiful wooden staircase with an ornate banister that looked like it came straight out of the movie *Meet Me in St. Louis*. Perhaps it was no accident that both *The Wizard of Oz* and *Meet Me in St. Louis* were my absolute favorite movies growing up.[*]

On the landing heading up the staircase was a door that, if opened, provided a bird's-eye view of the downstairs half bathroom. People using the bathroom were often quite concerned about this door. Why was that door there? What was the original layout of the house? We had theories but never really knew. The house had quirk and character.

The house was the *actual* poster child for the Herndon Historic Homes tour that took place annually. The front screen door of our house happened to be the logo for the tour.

Jackson Street also had a ton of history. At one time it had been a parsonage, an old schoolhouse, and in the 1970s, it had even briefly been home to Patch Adams and his Zanies while he was starting up his community hospital in West Virginia. But did my parents call attention to or celebrate these things at all? No. Instead, my dad installed a golden plaque on the house right by the front door that read "On this site in 1897, nothing happened."

My parents were married in the living room of the Jackson Street house on October 20, 1984, and I was christened in that same living room a year later.

It was the kind of house where people walked in the door without knocking, then went to the kitchen to fix themselves something to eat because they were at home there too. We *always* had someone staying with us. Whether it was a foreign exchange student, my sister and her friends, or one of the dozens of people over the years who was going

---

[*] Remember back in chapter 3 how I mentioned I had a bit of a thing for Judy Garland? And how I'd regularly dress up like her? Well, this only proved as more fodder for my method acting, and I would run in and out of the house reenacting different scenes from the movies.

DEAD BIRDS IN THE WALLS

through detox or had gotten out of rehab and had nowhere else to go . . . Jackson Street was where they came. Jackson Street was where they stayed.

Jackson Street was the hub for all things, and while it may have been a money pit at times, we loved it. So much.

Fast-forward to the summer of 1994: The house had received a lot of improvements over the years (mostly thanks to my drywalling dad), but a glaring issue was its lack of bathrooms. There was the weird-door-halfway-up-the-wall half bathroom downstairs and a full bathroom upstairs that also doubled as our laundry room. My sister, Bridgid, was in college, but we had my foster sister, Jamie, living with us at the time. With so many people staying in our house at any given moment, we needed to convert what was my mom's office into a large primary bathroom that would connect to my parents' room. They drew up the plans and got to work that fall.

OCTOBER 31, 1994—DEMO DAY, AGE 9

Having been a roofer and contractor for years, my dad "had a guy" for just about any job he needed done. (I promise my dad wasn't in the mob—not *that* kind of guy.) Dad brought in a demo crew to tear out walls, a crew to pull up carpet, and a crew to take everything down to the studs. When I say *take everything down to the studs*, we're talking the original circa-1900 plaster, horsehair insulation, and all. During the demo, the contractor's crew even found dead birds in the walls that had been there for who knows how long. But other than that, everything went relatively smoothly. Once the crew finished cleaning up the dust and debris, the room was down to its bare bones and the real renovation could begin.

That night my mom, dad, and I surveyed the progress, ate dinner, said our good nights, and went to bed. Tomorrow the fun could start!

Unbeknownst to all of us, that single, seemingly unimportant event would change our lives forever.

———

The next morning, my dad rolled over in bed and found my mom lying next to him foaming at the mouth. From my room, I awoke to the sound of my dad letting out a guttural scream. I ran in to see her barely breathing and barely conscious.

My mom was in full-blown pulmonary edema.

It's strange how some moments can either etch themselves into your brain or turn into a complete blur. This particular moment was both. Time seemed to move in slow motion, and yet, much of it felt blurry. I have flashes of standing in the doorway as my dad called 911 and frantically moved about. I remember crying. I remember not crying. I remember looking at my mom's face while white foam oozed from her lips and her eyes rolled back.

I remember it felt like hours, but it was really a few minutes before the paramedics arrived. I couldn't understand what was going on. I remember getting in the car with my dad and driving the 1.9 miles behind the ambulance all the way to the emergency room at Reston Hospital—the place where my mom happened to work as the night nursing supervisor. In the car, I have no idea if my dad and I spoke or if we remained silent. He doesn't remember either. My nine-year-old brain was frozen.

Mom was whisked back into a room, where the ER doctors immediately placed a chest tube in her. They called out medical phrases like "I need eighty ccs of this!" "Gimme four hundred ccs of that!" "We need a cart!" The hit show *ER* had just come on television that fall, and my parents were huge fans. It felt like I was watching an episode in real time.

I don't remember much about that time in the ER, but I do remember the vending machine snacks. I gorged myself on Doritos and honey buns while my mother's life hung by a thread. My mom was hooked up to an IV of saline while my dad put back a continuous drip of chocolate Yoo-hoo. While we didn't know what was going on, we did know it was serious.

Mom spent the next three weeks in the hospital acting as a human pincushion—poked and prodded as the medical staff tried to figure out what on earth could be ravaging her body. Her symptoms were all over the place. Respiratory issues, inflammation, irregular heart rate, pain. Her lead pulmonologist and primary care doctor had run countless tests, but nothing pinpointed the root cause. They couldn't determine why she wasn't able to breathe and why her symptoms kept changing so rapidly.

Dad was asked a million questions about her health leading up to the main event, to which he had no clear answers either. According to him, he'd never known Mom without some sort of knee brace, wrist brace, or random pain issue. But never anything respiratory.

Once Dad began to recount the day's events—the demolition and cleanup of the upstairs of the home—things started to unravel.

The doctors suggested testing the plaster dust, the horsehair insulation, and even the dead birds to see if they'd caused something. All these initial tests came back *relatively* normal. Samples were sent to labs across the country, yielding nothing but "inconclusive" results. The more they investigated, though, the more convinced they became that a toxin from something in those walls had invaded her lungs. But why just hers? Why not my dad's lungs? Why not mine? What made Mom's condition so unique?

Eventually, the doctors reached their limit and referred us to the Johns Hopkins Hospital, where they ran more blood work and more CT scans and more MRIs and more X-rays and nearly every medical test known to modern medicine at the time. They, too, couldn't find a thing. Johns Hopkins then sent us to the Mayo Clinic, where they did the same thing. Nothing. Not a single clear answer. To say we were feeling frustrated, terrified, and defeated is an understatement.

At nine years old, I could see the fear, anxiety, and trepidation written all over my parents' faces. My dad's firm voice held a hint of curtness as he tried to answer my incessant questions.

Me: Why is Mommy sick?
Dad: Some bad stuff got in her lungs.
Me: Will Mommy get better?
Dad: We don't know.
Me: What's her sickness called?
Dad: We don't know.
Me: Is it contagious?
Dad: No, honey.
Me: What's going to happen?
Dad: We don't know.

My mom, ever the optimist, would take me in her arms and rock me like a baby, stroking my hair and singing "My Favorite Things" softly in my ear, as though I was the one who was sick and needed comfort. Yet I could hear that air of concern in her voice, and even more so, I could see it in her eyes.

All I wanted to do was fix it. I'd offer to bring Mom breakfast in bed, refill her Diet Coke cup, or watch TV with her on the couch. I felt helpless.

My older sister, Bridgid, was away at college at the time, and as I sat in the next room, I could hear Mom and Dad on the phone trying to catch her up as much as possible without scaring her. In those moments, my parents worked so hard to strike the most difficult balance.

In one appointment, Mom's lead pulmonologist, Dr. Reynolds, said, "Look, I think we've exhausted all of our options here. There's a hospital out in Denver, Colorado, called National Jewish Center for Immunology and Respiratory Medicine. Their respiratory and immunology centers are some of the best in the country, and I think it's the next best option for you. If we could figure it out here, we would have by now. And I'm afraid we're losing time."

The problem was, a trip to Denver would not be quick, easy, or cheap. We absolutely didn't have the money to go. We'd been struggling financially for a while, and a cross-country road trip wasn't in the cards. I sat and overheard my parents talking through the logistics, trying every which way to make the trip work.

Finally, I remember my dad saying, "Look, Lynda, we're going. We have a Shell gas card and an Exxon gas card . . . If we have to eat at gas stations along the way, we will. We're going to Denver." I watched as my parents held hands and prayed, believing it was going to be okay . . .

God, grant us the serenity to accept the things we cannot change, the courage to change the things we can, and the wisdom to know the difference. Amen.

6

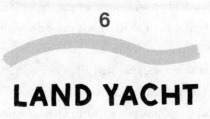

LAND YACHT

MARCH 1, 1995

*First the doctor told me the good news. I was
going to have a disease named after me.*

STEVE MARTIN

In March 1995, with a whole lot of faith and a little bit of gas credit, we packed up our old Jamboree motor home, which aptly donned the license plate "LND YAHT." We made arrangements with my school so I could be out of class for a while, then headed to Denver for the foreseeable future.

The day we planned to leave, both my mom and I were antsy and very much ready to leave. We were waiting on my dad, which *never* happened. This was a Buckley Family First. For a reason he couldn't explain, Dad insisted on waiting for the mail to come before we hit the road. The mail arrived, and in it just happened to be a check for $2,500 made out to my mom from the VVA. There was nothing written on the memo line, so the reason for the check was not clear—but my dad looked at my mom and said, "Well, looks like God heard our prayers. This'll pay for the trip."

And we hit the road.

It took about five days to drive out to Denver. I enjoyed any opportunity we got to take the motor home somewhere, but in particular, I loved this trip out West. I mean, part of it was because I was nine and was about to miss a whole lot of school, so that was awesome; but the main reason was because I got to spend the majority of the time up front in the copilot's seat right next to my dad. My mom spent most of the ride in the back, sleeping, reading, or crocheting. But Dad and I were in our own little world in the cockpit.

We played the license plate game, searching for each letter of the alphabet. We played I spy and told jokes. I spent hours jabbering away about who knows what, then I'd color. But my *favorite* thing was talking on the CB (citizens band) radio. The CB radio allowed us to communicate with just about any trucker nearby, and we'd only use our code names. My code name? Little Pony. Dad's code name? Old Goat. We talked to some drivers on the road through multiple states, and I'd ask them all sorts of logistical questions about the loads they were carrying or where they were going or if they liked donuts or bagels better. I took CB radio talk very seriously.

On day four, just outside Denver, we pulled into a little RV park in Golden, Colorado, to park in what was to be our home for the foreseeable future. The day we arrived was absolutely beautiful! It was sunny! And in the sixties! Unseasonably warm for Colorado in March, we were told. We grilled a little dinner on a charcoal grill with a picturesque view of the Rocky Mountains before us. We decided to go to bed early that night so we could get up at the crack of dawn and drive into Denver for the first day of testing at the hospital.

But when we woke up, it was no longer beautiful! And sunny! And in the sixties! Or unseasonably warm for Colorado in March! Instead, it was twenty-five degrees outside, and there was a foot and a half of snow on the ground. We were in disbelief. How does this happen so quickly? Thankfully my dad was a prepared man. He happened to have ice scrapers and a small shovel in a storage compartment, so he and I got up to dig out the RV because it was our only vehicle for the trip. This was the start of our new daily routine: pack up the RV in Golden, then drive it thirty minutes into downtown Denver to take Mom to the hospital.

For over three weeks, we repeated our routine. Pack up the motor home. Drive to the hospital. Check Mom in for testing. Sit in the motor home in the parking lot for hours. Eat bad hospital food. Stare into the abyss. Mom was a human test subject being put on every machine they had, and I think they even invented machines just for her visit. What a delight for her.

I'd call my teachers on our suitcase-sized car phone (that plugged into the cigarette lighter!) to get my homework for the day, then I would send postcards to my friends, color, or play games. Sometimes we went into the hospital to be with Mom while she did her tests. Despite her being hooked up to so many things, she was always trying to smile, crack a joke, or make light of the situation. She and Dad would do bits pretending she was prepping for a trip to the moon or on her last leg of the Tour de France.

I put on a strong face for my parents when they joked, but I was terrified. All the cords, wires, and needles, along with the endless stream of nurses and doctors and specialists moving in and out of the room using words I didn't understand, was too much for me to bear.

In the rare moments I was alone, I often fought back tears. I had started to come to terms with what we were facing. On our third or fourth night in Denver, after we drove back to the RV park for the night, I told my parents I was "going for a hike." There was a small mountain (more like a glorified large hill with some rocks) in the middle of the RV park, and I told them I wanted to hike to the top. They let me go alone, so I grabbed my flashlight, my Walkman, and my Green Day *Dookie* cassette tape and said I'd be back in a bit.

When I hit play, Green Day themselves seemed to be narrating my every emotion with every step I took. I was "Having a Blast," I felt like a "Chump," and by the time I got to the top of the mountain, I heard "Welcome to Paradise." It was the first moment in nearly four months when I was able to really process all that was happening. While I didn't fully understand it yet, I was smart enough to realize that we hadn't traveled all the way to Denver for the flu or some random infection. This was serious. I broke down and cried like I hadn't cried before. Needless to say, I was a "Basket Case."*

The longer we stayed in Denver, the more dumbfounded by my mom's case the doctors, nurses, and specialists became. It seemed like her symptoms kept changing hour by hour, and her condition kept getting worse. Like all the other medical professionals we'd seen, they could not pinpoint what was causing it.

Eventually, while grasping at straws, the doctors landed on a few likely diagnoses. First, they diagnosed her with a severe case of constrictive bronchiolitis, a small airway fibrotic respiratory disease that eventually obstructs both lungs. In layman's terms, her lungs were suffocating her. The opposite of what lungs are created to do. Most people who are diagnosed with it are given a survival rate under two and a half years. The other diagnosis the doctors landed on was an extremely rare autoimmune disease known as granulomatosis with

---

* I enjoy knowing that these references are very niche and that fans of '90s alternative music will very much appreciate them.

polyangiitis† (formerly known as Wegener's disease)—a disorder that causes inflammation of the blood vessels in your nose, sinuses, throat, lungs, and kidneys. Again, in layman's terms: it slowed blood flow to the organs, causing them to eventually fail. The other diagnosis didn't even have a name; they just knew the disease was eating away at Mom from the inside out.

The doctors said that about four other people in the entire *world* had ever been diagnosed with anything similar to what she was experiencing—which meant that treatment, for the most part, would be like throwing spaghetti at a wall and seeing what would stick.

The combination of diagnoses left a grim prognosis for my mom. After a few really difficult conversations, the doctors in Denver told her she probably had around two years left to live, at most. My parents were faced with impossible choices and overwhelming odds.

Mom and Dad weren't sure how to tell me this news. Ultimately, they decided it was best not to share Mom's diagnosis with me in order to protect me from the very long (or short) road ahead of us. All I was told was that Mom was sick and that she'd be sick for the rest of her life; I simply didn't know that "the rest of her life" was not likely to be a long time. Not until I started writing this book did I finally have the long-awaited conversation with my dad about the truth of what they were carrying. They knew there was no cure for the disease, and the only thing doctors knew to do was to treat her symptoms. Doctors began flooding her body with every medication they could think of. They also suggested we look into some alternative forms of medicine because, hey, we had nothing to lose.

† I dare you to say that three times fast.

My mom had been placed on prednisone because it was the only medication that kept her breathing. It subsequently became the drug we loved to hate because she would stay on that drug for the next eight years. The long-term side effects of prednisone included skin that felt like tissue paper, and she got the very common "moon face" along with a host of other issues. But it kept her breathing. Doctors still had very little clue regarding the cause of her sudden illness. While her symptoms were unlike anything they'd seen before, they weren't giving up.

After a month, we loaded up LND YAHT and drove home from Denver, taking every minute to process all that had happened. Our lives had changed so much in such a short amount of time. Once at home, Mom was placed on disability from her job at Reston Hospital.

———

As other issues cropped up, the doctors dug further into Mom's medical history—more specifically, about her time serving in Vietnam. Prior to serving, Mom had been a young, healthy, active woman who ran marathons, hiked mountains, and lived a life of constant activity and adventure. In the years after returning home from Vietnam, emotional and mental effects aside, she had a host of "little issues" that, on the surface, seemed superficial. She constantly had heating pads or knee braces or wrist braces on because of aches and pains that seemed abnormal for someone her age. It was almost as if her body was beginning to send little messages that something was going on.

This information led doctors down a rabbit hole looking for clues, and the more they uncovered, the more evidence led them to one source: her exposure in Vietnam to the chemical known as Agent Orange.

A quick history for those who don't know: Agent Orange was a "tactical use" herbicide and defoliant chemical widely used by the US military during the Vietnam War as a part of its herbicidal warfare program. Herbicidal warfare was designed to, essentially, wipe out the plant-based ecosystem of a region. What this did was disrupt food production and destroy plants that might provide cover for enemy forces. Several "Rainbow Herbicides" were sprayed throughout Southeast Asia during the Vietnam War, from 1961 to 1971. As you can surmise, this tactic ended up being a terrible idea.

My mom's team of doctors began looking into the 71st Evacuation Hospital where she was stationed, and as they suspected, the 71st had been defoliated daily with Agent Orange, Agent Blue, and Agent White. For the entire year she was in Vietnam, she—and everyone else around her—was breathing in and absorbing these chemicals. Every doctor assigned to my mom's case came to the same conclusion: A preponderance of evidence showed that her exposure to those chemicals was, without a doubt, the root cause of her illnesses.

Now, how do you explain all this to a nine-year-old? I remember this is how the doctor explained it to me: "We all have an immune system, right? Think of your immune system as a safe with a padlock on it. Yes, some illnesses (robbers, in this analogy) might come into your body and crack open the safe for a little while, but then your immune system fights back and kicks the robbers out! Now, imagine that your immune system is cracked open by the ultimate locksmith (such as Agent Orange), but the locksmith decides to leave that safe door ajar for the next twenty years. Eventually the wrong things will get inside very easily."

Enter: toxic dust and dead birds in the walls of a nearly hundred-year-old home.

We had a set of diagnoses and a root cause. It felt like progress. But we also had a large stack of substantial medical bills. Since Mom was a veteran, she should get coverage for all this . . . right? Wrong. There was one big problem.

At the time, the VA (Veterans Affairs) department was barely talking about Agent Orange and the health effects it had not only on the women and men who served in Vietnam but also on their children. Only eight maladies were eligible for compensation in regard to Agent Orange exposure, and essentially all of them were forms of cancer. Mom didn't have cancer, which meant Mom didn't get any medical or financial support from the VA. Zero. Zip. Zilch. Nada.

Despite being unable to get any compensation for her Agent Orange illness, and after a lot of campaigning from her doctors, Mom was finally able to get an intake appointment at the VA hospital for basic VA benefits.

As she and my dad sat in the meeting with the intake officer, painstakingly filling out forms, the officer began explaining the benefits Mom would be eligible for. "Mrs. Buckley, you will have access to VA doctors, the VA pharmacy, and other basic services here at the VA hospital," the intake officer continued. "And, should you pass, you are entitled to a funeral with full military honors including a flag-draped casket and a twenty-one-gun salute."

My mom, with all the energy she could muster, sat straight up, scooched her chair forward, leaned her arms on the desk, looked the intake officer dead in the eyes, and said, "Sir, I'll take the flag-draped casket . . . I earned that. But you can take the twenty-one guns and shove them where the sun don't shine.‡ I'll have twenty-one doves released, thank you."

It was all my dad could do not to suffocate from his stifled laughter. Because if he didn't laugh, he was pretty sure he'd cry.

---

‡ I believe what she said may have been a bit more . . . colorful.

7

CONSTRICTIVE BRONCHIOLITIS AND GRANULOMATOSIS WITH POLYANGIITIS*

NOVEMBER 1994–NOVEMBER 2002

A man with his health has a thousand
dreams; a man without it has only one.

UNKNOWN

Mom may have rejected her death sentence, but unfortunately, she was still facing a life sentence. The thing is, when you're sick, the only thing you really care about is not being sick anymore. And that's not just because being sick is miserable. It's also because, as we came to learn, when you're sick for a long time, every other area of your life starts to fall apart too.

---

* No, really. Say it three times fast. Go on. Try it.

The years after Mom's diagnosis were fraught with challenges. More often than not, we felt like pinballs being bounced from slingshots to bumpers to flippers as we tried to keep Mom (and us) out of the trough. It was a lot. She had her good days, she had her bad days, and she had her "We need to call 911" days. There was no in-between.

While she and my dad continued to keep the ticking clock a secret from me, I was a perceptive kid. I saw the toll her illness was taking on her, my dad, and our entire family. The physical pieces of her illness were hard enough, but the cost in every other area of our lives wasn't the part any of us could have predicted.

FINANCIAL

The trip to Denver was covered with gas cards and a surprise check from the VVA, but everything afterward had to be taken a day, and sometimes a moment, at a time. When Mom first got sick, she was able to go on disability from her job as the night nursing supervisor at Reston Hospital. However, that short-term disability eventually went to long-term disability, and it quickly ran out. We not only lost Mom's income but we also lost our health insurance, so my dad ended up having to get a job as a customer service manager at Hechinger, a big-box home improvement store with a bunch of locations in the area. However, even with Dad's Hechinger health insurance, we were still required to pay between 20 and 25 percent of every doctor's visit, treatment, test, lab, prescription, and hospital stay. And, the thing was, Mom had a lot of doctor's visits, treatments, tests, labs, prescriptions, and hospital stays. By the fall of 1996, we were drowning in medical debt.

It should surprise no one that the VA was entirely unhelpful. No matter what we did, Mom was denied any veteran disability from the

VA for her illness. Every "DENIED" letter we received in the mail felt like a punch in the gut. In the VA claims legal world, in order to receive benefits, the burden of proof is on each veteran to prove their medical condition is "at least as likely as not" related to their military service. Yet, despite the "preponderance of evidence" (another VA term) in favor of Mom's illness being directly connected to her exposure to Agent Orange, her claims were repeatedly denied. It didn't matter what doctor's notes, lab reports, or test results we showed them, the VA would say something to the effect of "Agent Orange didn't do this."

Mom's case wasn't unique, as literally thousands of other Vietnam veterans were denied benefits for their illnesses related to Agent Orange. However, our frustration only increased when we learned that the head of the committee looking at Mom's case was one of the same women who'd "had it out for her" back in the early '80s when Mom's book, *Home Before Morning*, was released. We knew what was happening to Mom was not only wrong but also illegal. Mom had quite a few advocates at the VA fighting for her every which way they could, but it often amounted to nothing. Additionally, the appeals process was brutally long, and bureaucratic red tape got in the way of any attempt at progress.

In the meantime, we were hemorrhaging money.

Eventually, Mom's illness affected her mobility to the point that she couldn't physically get around anymore. She'd had two hip replacements and three (yes, three) knee replacements. Every joint in her body was deteriorating more rapidly than we could keep up with. Getting up the stairs in the Jackson Street home was now nearly impossible, so my parents were faced with two choices:

1. Convert the downstairs dining room into a bedroom.
2. Sell the Jackson Street house and buy a ranch home in Ocean City, Maryland.

The first option was a no-go. Not only did that logistically not make sense, but the cost would be more than Mom and Dad could figure. Upfitting the dining room into a bedroom and then somehow putting a full bath downstairs was out of the question. They submitted an application to the VA benefits department for a chairlift for our staircase, only to have that denied as well.

This left only the second option. Mom and Dad had kept this idea a secret from me and gone on an "anniversary trip" to Ocean City to look around at houses. They'd found a nice neighborhood with ranch homes that had easy golf cart access to grocery stores and restaurants. After discussion and prayer, they said, "Well, if God wants us to move here, he's gotta make it happen. But if he doesn't, then he's gotta do a miracle."

A week before they'd planned to put Jackson Street on the market, Mom's friend from Vietnam, Richard, knocked on the door. Richard also happened to work for the VVA.

"We got you a chairlift, Lynda," Richard said.

Mom's eyes welled up with tears and gratitude as Richard walked in the door and pointed a technician toward the staircase.

"It goes right over there," he directed.

Somehow, Richard (and God) had arranged for a miracle to happen. The very miracle Mom and Dad needed to know we were supposed to stay in Herndon.

Then in 1999, Mom was finally approved for minimal VA benefits solely related to her diagnosed PTSD. This service connection eased some burden but not nearly enough to make a significant dent. Meanwhile, my parents continued fighting to get her Agent Orange appeal approved. Each time they were told to "wait to hear from us."

That day would never come.

FAMILIAL

Ever since Mom came home from Vietnam, her relationship with her family had been complicated. With the exception of her dad, no one in her family particularly wanted to hear much about her experience. Like nearly all veterans, Mom came home from the war a *very* different person, which was hard for everyone, her family included. It didn't help that Mom returned with PTSD, depression, and a good ol' classic case of alcoholism. Despite getting therapy and eventually getting sober in May 1983, the family was never the same after that.

When Mom became ill, her family was strangely and immediately suspicious. The line of questioning as to "What's going on?" and "Why is she in the hospital so much?" and "Why is she on all these medications?" was rapid-fire. We were doing the best we could to understand all the ins and outs of her illness, but since we hardly understood it ourselves, explaining her condition to everyone else felt impossible. Pretty soon, her family started to wonder if she really *was* sick or if she was somehow relapsing to her old days before she got sober. Her cousins, her siblings, and even her own mother began to question her medication plan, asking if she really needed to be on all the steroids or if she was just using the illness as an excuse to get attention. Her family started to pull away—not only from her but from all of us. I watched in disbelief as it slowly broke my mom's heart.

Her relationship with Poppy remained strong, and he was the glue that held what was left of the family together. Then in 1996, Poppy's health rapidly declined, and we knew our time with him was running out. For whatever reason, the rest of Mom's family did whatever they could to keep her away from Poppy. When Poppy went into the hospital in November, the family told Mom she shouldn't come to the hospital "in her condition" to see her father. My dad ever so firmly and lovingly said, "Absolutely not. We're going to the hospital." Then he put us in the car to go see Poppy.

When we arrived at the hospital, Mom's family was livid that we were there. I was eleven as I watched them yell at her that she shouldn't be there. With her head high and her mouth shut, Mom hobbled on her crutches right past them into the room. I watched as she held her dear daddy's hand—singing over him, talking to him, telling him over and over again that she loved him.

We hugged him. We cried. We laughed.

Poppy died the next day.

Poppy's death was the final unraveling of it all. Any semblance of unity left in the family passed away with Poppy.

Mom continually did everything she could to reach out to her family, even when she felt at her worst. But any and all attempts were only met with contempt. One day, I went out to check the mail and discovered a card addressed to Mom from a family member. Mom had wondered why this family member (or anyone, really) hadn't been by to visit her during her illness, especially since Mom had reached out to check on them when their uncle was sick. Mom figured her family was just busy. I ran upstairs to Mom's room with the card, knowing she would be so excited to hear from family. She opened it up, and inside was a "Cheery Get Well Thoughts" card with a panda playing among butterflies on the front. A note fell out of the card, and Mom began to read it.

Lynda,

It was nice to hear from you last night. I'm sorry that you are still having problems and have been in the hospital for three weeks. I appreciate you and your friends taking the time to see my father and offering our family assistance during his illness. What I would like for you to do is get your own life in order. Hopefully, the doctors will be able to help you and get you off the steroids. Believe me, you could not do anything for my family in your present condition. More importantly, you need to put all your efforts into making amends with your family. I'm very disturbed by your actions toward your family. Do something before it's too late.

I watched as Mom slowly collapsed onto her pillow, tears streaming down her face. She sobbed and sobbed. I looked over at my dad, who was running to Mom to comfort her. We made eye contact, and I could see the rage building in his eyes. He was furious.

From that day forward, he vowed to protect her peace. Nothing got past my dad. No letter, no phone call, and no visitor got to my mom without him screening it first. A few weeks later, Mom received a letter in the mail from one of her sisters. Knowing the pain of rejection Mom had felt from her family, Dad wouldn't even open the letter or show it to Mom. He wrote "return to sender" on the envelope and popped it back in the mailbox, never even mentioning it to her.

To anyone on the outside, Dad might've seemed overprotective or controlling. But that wasn't the case. In order for Mom to fight as best as she could, Dad did whatever *he* could to keep any negativity and unnecessary stress out of her life.

Losing the love and support of her family was one of the most crushing blows for Mom, not only because it was yet another loss for her but also because it meant I lost them too. I was somehow roped into all of it, and I lost my grandmother, my aunts, my cousins whom I'd been so close to, and all my extended family. They were now no longer a part of our lives. Not only that, but they would say things about us, about *me*, that just weren't true. We'd suffered so much, and this reality felt so overwhelming.

While Mom's illness took so much from us, this piece was easily the most painful for all of us. When you're hurting, more often than not, the only thing you want and need is the love of family. And being ostracized by those closest to you is salt on an open wound.

Mom was never healed from this portion of her pain. I lost contact with my aunts and cousins for decades. A few years ago, I made the conscious decision to forgive them. I let some of them know directly. Others, I let God know. While I've been able to restore only one relationship, that is enough for me.

MARITAL

Chronic illnesses are incredibly difficult on marriages. Many marriages don't make it, or the caretaking spouse becomes resentful and distant. By the grace of God, that wasn't my parents' story.

From the time they said "I do," Mom and Dad were put through test after test—yet their love only grew stronger. When Mom became ill, Dad shifted into the roles of not only husband but also protector, provider, and caretaker.

More than anyone else, Dad had a front-row seat to Mom's daily battles. So often she would say to him, "I'm so sorry, Tom. You didn't ask to take on my burdens. You didn't sign up for all this." And he'd lovingly respond with "Yes, I did. This is what I signed up for when I said in sickness and in health, for richer or for poorer, for better or for worse, 'til death do us part. You'd do the same if it were me."

Much to my chagrin, they managed to keep their spark alive, doing whatever they could to gross me out as much as humanly possible. They would go on dates, even if that meant "dating" at home. They were intentional about alone time, and when circumstances allowed it, they would get a weekend or two away alone each year. They also were incredibly affectionate, always sneaking kisses or little butt smacks. (I have VHS tapes of my dad filming my mom's butt as she walked away.) Also, it was not uncommon to be sitting at the breakfast table only to see my mom wink at my dad and say, "Thanks for last night, honey." To which I would immediately vomit in my mouth.

As cliché as it might seem, they treated each day as a gift because they were hyperaware of no guaranteed tomorrows. Dad often said that because they lived so "in the moment," he would lose track of what day it was, what month it was, and even what year it was. Everything blurred together.

Even with their intentionality in making their marriage as strong as could be, the obstacles they faced began to wear on my dad. Of course he loved his wife. Of course he wanted to care for her and protect her. But the reality was, he was exhausted. He was working nearly a hundred hours a week, staying up late (if not all night), and caring for Mom. He strove to keep them both active in my life and my sister's life while she was in college. He even worked to maintain friendships and participate in AA. Trying to keep our lives afloat while we paid off medical bills was hard enough. He wasn't taking care of himself.

Dad eventually sought counseling, and the counselor said to him, "Tom, if you keep this up, your daughters are going to lose both parents. Do what you must to take care of *you*."

That night, after coming home and talking with Mom, he agreed to move into our guest room. Since Mom was up all hours of the night, Dad was hardly sleeping. Having his own space would give him much-needed rest. From that point forward, Dad would spend some time each night with Mom in their room snuggling, talking, and watching *ER* or *Hill Street Blues* or *NYPD Blue*. Then he'd retreat to the guest room to sleep. Each morning he'd take some time to pray, meditate, and practice gratitude so he would be mentally, spiritually, and physically ready for whatever the day brought.

That ended up being the best decision he could have made at the time.

His role as protector came in many forms. Not only did he protect her from those who sought to take her down but he also protected her physically. This came to a head one night while we went out for ice cream.

It was a beautiful summer night, and my junior year of high school was about to start. Mom had one of her better days and was up and moving around more than normal, so we thought we'd celebrate by going out for ice cream. Dad, Mom, and I drove to Baskin-Robbins and stood in line to order. The place was mostly empty except for a couple of employees and three young people in their late teens or early twenties who'd walked in behind us. Dad and I ordered while Mom stood next to us—leaning on her crutches and making friends with the employee scooping her ice cream. Anywhere we went, Mom made friends. She was always getting to know the person behind the cash register or the waitress in the restaurant or the ice cream scooper at Baskin-Robbins. She'd call them by their name, ask them about their lives, and by the time she'd leave, they'd basically be family. Mom would find herself invited to their wedding or baby shower. She was a stranger to no one.

As Mom continued to laugh and talk with the woman working, Dad and I laughed, sighed, and said, "Take your time, Lynda, we'll be in the car with our ice cream." She chuckled and said, "I'll be there shortly!" knowing all the while that she'd be out in about twenty minutes.

Dad and I walked to the car and watched as Mom laughed and smiled with the Baskin-Robbins employee. A few minutes went by, and we saw Mom, as fast as she physically could, hobbling out on her crutches with a look of utter terror on her face. She was pale and shaking uncontrollably. She started to cry.

"We have to leave," she said. "We need to go now."

"What happened, Lynda?" Dad replied.

Out of breath and through sobs of tears, she said, "Those kids behind me in line . . . they were angry . . . they . . . got in my face . . . they cursed me out . . . they called me a cripple and said horrible things . . . they said I was holding up the line and that I better get out of their way. I . . . I was . . . I was just trying to be kind to the workers . . ."

The look on my dad's face turned from concern to utter rage. He got out of the car and walked over to the kids sitting down at a table outside. I watched as he placed his hand on the shoulder of one of the boys and said, "Excuse me." In a flash, one of the other boys stood up and punched my dad in the face. They knocked Dad to the ground and began to beat the ever-loving mess out of him. He did all he could to defend himself and fight back, but the three kids had him surrounded—kicking him in the ribs, punching him, and slamming him to the ground.

Mom and I screamed. Baskin-Robbins employees came outside, people ran over to pull these kids off of Dad, and someone called 911. The scene was horrific. I saw Dad's bloodied face on the ground, but he was just angered all the more. I couldn't stop crying, and all I could hear was the sound of my own screams.

By the time the police arrived, someone had detained the kids and taken statements. Dad was taken to the hospital. He'd suffered multiple broken ribs and was covered in cuts and bruises.

On top of everything we'd been through, watching my dad be assaulted in that way was the cherry on top of an already awful season.

AA

Early on in Mom's illness, getting to AA meetings became extremely difficult. This began to have a serious effect on her—but it didn't last long. On one particular Tuesday night, a bunch of Mom and Dad's friends showed up at the house and walked in to bring an AA meeting to Mom. The next night, they showed up again. Then, on Saturday night, they showed up again.

That's when the Jackson Street AA group was born.

For over eight years, the Jackson Street group met in our home three nights a week. Whether we were there or not, anywhere from ten to one hundred people would be in our living room sharing their stories, fellowshipping, and drinking *so much coffee*. It became a group of people that held our family up when we so badly needed support. It gave Mom and Dad the community they had missed.

But the community wasn't without its flaws. There came a time in Mom's illness when many of her own friends thought my dad couldn't take care of her.

One day, Dad was taken out to lunch by one of his best friends. Over coffee and burgers, his friend said to him, "Tom, the guys and I think you need to put Lynda in some kind of institution or group home where she can be properly cared for."

In that moment, Dad wanted to reach across the table and punch his friend in the face. But instead, he took a deep breath and said, "Jim, you have no idea. You have no idea what's going on. As long as I have breath in my lungs, Lynda is going to stay in her home with her stuff and her bed and her child." And he got up and walked out.

A few years later, Jim's wife was diagnosed with cancer. Jim called Dad to meet for a cup of coffee, and as they sat down, Jim looked at Dad and said, "Tom, I'm sorry. I had no idea. I apologize for suggesting how to handle Lynda's illness. I get it now. I hope you can forgive me."

MOTHERHOOD

When Mom received her diagnosis, the first thing that came to her mind was her fear of not seeing me grow up. She said to Dad that she would fight as hard as she could to be active in my life, to participate in things with me, to see me do the things I loved, and to not miss out on a single moment. This wasn't anything I was made aware of at the time, but now that I look back, I can see how she fought through the pain in order to be present.

I had to grow up a whole lot faster than most kids my age. My parents had to teach me how to drive a car at age eleven just in case something happened and I needed to get Mom to the hospital. I knew how to administer a nebulizer treatment and countless medications. I knew how to do CPR. Our lives revolved around doctor's appointments and hospital stays and surgeries.

Mom wasn't able to physically do the kinds of things most moms did, but she found ways to connect with me anyway. Our home was always open for my friends, and Jackson Street became "the hangout house" everyone wanted to come to. My friends wouldn't even knock on the door because they knew they'd be welcomed in with a hug and a snack, even if I wasn't there. She held my friends as they cried over breakups or took them in when they were dealing with family drama. She never judged or offered unsolicited advice; she just listened and shared. She answered any questions we had honestly. No topic was off-limits.

She would take me to the nail salon to get our nails done, and

I'd listen as she practiced speaking Vietnamese with our favorite nail technicians. She'd take me for Diet Cokes and yogurt parfaits from McDonald's. She'd take me to the mall and ride around on her Amigo scooter, driving way too fast and taking out racks of clothing in the process.

But we really connected over our love of music, singing, and performing. Whether I was preparing for a chorus concert, play, or performance of some kind, she was there to help me every step of the way. I was an avid golfer growing up (thanks to my dad) and played competitively from late elementary school through high school. She had grown to love golf as well, and my dad had even come up with ways for her to play despite her limited mobility. But no matter what, she was at nearly every golf match and tournament I ever played in— driving a golf cart, following me along.

She loved taking my friends and me to concerts. My first concert was Brian McKnight, and I remember her screaming the lyrics to "Back at One" at the top of her lungs.

Or there was the time she took my friends and me to see NSYNC. She was more excited than we were (and we were *really* excited)—so much so that she went to Deb Shops and bought herself an outfit for the evening: a gold glitter tank top, a pleather coat, and a pair of printed snakeskin pleather pants. It was peak embarrassing. There we were: my four friends, me, and my decked-out mother in an Amigo scooter, arriving at the NSYNC concert in style.

Mere moments into the show, though, after the arena went dark, sudden flashes of lights and fireworks erupted as Justin, JC, Joey, Lance, and Chris took the stage. I screamed in teenage delight as the opening bars to "I Want You Back" played, but when I looked over to my left toward my mom, I couldn't see her anywhere. Her Amigo scooter was there unattended, and I knew something had happened.

I started to panic. I told my friends I'd be right back, then left the seating area in the arena to look for her. I got about fifteen steps out and found Mom on the floor in front of the concessions stand, rocking back and forth and crying. She sat with her hands on her head, screaming, "It will all be over soon."

I leaned down and tapped her on the shoulder. "Mom? Are you okay?"

She looked up at me in horror. "Who are you? *Who are you?* Get down! Are you crazy? The Viet Cong are firing on us! We're under attack!" she screamed.

"What? Mom, it's me. Molly. The Viet Cong aren't firing—"

She cut me off. "*Get down!* I'll ask again! Who are you?" she cried.

"I'm . . . your daughter. We are at an NSYNC concert, Mom. We're at the MCI Center in Washington, DC."

"Stop lying!" she screamed.

She continued to rock back and forth, holding her head and crying. I had no idea what to do. I'd heard her talk of her PTSD episodes and flashbacks, but I'd never seen one so severe. The sounds and lights had triggered something in her, and I had no idea how to snap her out of it. But even worse, she'd gotten out of the arena so fast that she'd fallen down and couldn't physically get herself back up.

The adrenaline in her body kicked in, and by the time she calmed down and came back to reality, I couldn't pick her up. I had to ask a security guard to help me get her back to our seats. She had no memory or recollection of what had happened, having completely blacked out. When I tried to explain to her what I'd seen, she sat and cried and apologized over and over.

We both were so shaken we couldn't even enjoy the rest of the concert. My friends hadn't a clue what had taken place.

As I saw the toll her illness and her PTSD took on her life, I became overwhelmed with fear of the unknown and fear of what would come.

It all felt so unfair.

Mom's illness took a lot from us. It took our money, it took our family, it took our friends, and it took away any semblance of a normal life.

But the one thing it didn't take was our sense of humor.

8

THE GROTTO OF LOURDES

FALL 1998

> With the fearful strain that is on me night
> and day, if I did not laugh, I should die.
>
> ABRAHAM LINCOLN

While my parents did their best to shield me from the realities and grim details of what we were facing as a family, not everything was doom and gloom. Our home was constantly filled with laughter. We were a boisterous, loud-laughing family that could find the humor and joy in almost any situation—even if that situation (or the humor, for that matter) was borderline inappropriate. Let's be honest: When you bring together two recovering alcoholic Irish Catholics in the covenant of holy matrimony, hilarity is bound to ensue. Not to mention, nurses already have a bit of a macabre sense of humor when it comes to medical stuff. If my parents were able to make light of something with regard to my mom's illnesses, you bet they embraced the opportunity.

Our family believed laughter, sent straight from God, was the best medicine, and we did whatever we could to overdose on it.

We also tried to get out of town whenever possible. My mom loved the outdoors, and my dad exercised everything within his power to make sure she did what she loved. Since money was always tight, we vacationed by packing up LND YAHT and driving it to different campgrounds up and down the East Coast. Every fall, we'd travel up to Hershey, Pennsylvania, for an annual camping trip with my parents' AA friends. No matter how sick Mom was, we tried to never miss a trip. We'd bring every medicine and every machine along with us because despite the challenges they brought, those trips brought life to our weary souls.

On one particular trip in the fall of 1998, we were driving back home from Hershey on Route 15 in Maryland. As we approached Emmitsburg, my dad excitedly turned to my mom and said, "Honey! Look! Just up ahead is the Grotto of Our Lady of Lourdes—we *have* to go. We've passed it a half dozen times over the years and have never stopped. I mean, we've taken you to spiritual healers, Indigenous healers, and natural healers. We've done traditional Chinese medicine, Reiki, massage, meditation, aromatherapy, hypnotherapy, naturopathy, acupuncture, acupressure, reflexology, and eating vegetables. But you know what we haven't tried? Holy water! *That* will be the thing to fix all this."

My mom could sense that my dad was just trying to find humor and a soupçon of levity amid a dark situation while also taking the opportunity to poke fun at their strict Catholic upbringings. She turned to him, looked him straight in the eye, and said, "Take the exit."

My best friend Becca had joined me on this particular trip, and let's just say that two middle school girls weren't exactly jazzed about making a pit stop at the Grotto of Our Lady of Lourdes. But it was a chance to get some fresh air, so we pulled in and parked. My dad got my mom settled in her wheelchair, and Becca and I grabbed a couple of large plastic pitchers from LND YAHT's cabinets and set off in search of holy water. Now, I should note that my mom could walk sometimes. She mostly got around with crutches or an upside-down golf putter she used as a cane, but walking long distances or uphill was out of the question. That's why we always had a wheelchair or a motorized scooter with us to make it easier for her to get around.

The Grotto of Our Lady of Lourdes was really a beautiful place, but it certainly was not what we had envisioned in any way, shape, or form. The actual grotto part of the Grotto of Our Lady of Lourdes sat at the top of a hill, and from the parking lot up to it was a long, steep, paved walkway. Becca and I ran to the top and watched my dad push my mom up the hill. As he pushed her, they began to note the long line of beautiful brick archways and mini grottos that featured the various stations of the cross.

Below the first station of the cross, emblazoned on a large bronze plaque, was the name of a Baltimore Irish family who donated the money for said bronze plaque in order to be forever commemorated.

The next station of the cross featured an additional bronze plaque with a different Baltimore Irish family who donated the money for said bronze plaque.

The third station of the cross featured yet another bronze plaque with a different Baltimore Irish family who donated more money for said bronze plaque.

And so on, and so on. This went on for all fourteen stations of the cross.

The entire way my dad pushed my mom up the hill, he cracked old Irish Catholic jokes in her ear—and the more he joked, the more she just egged him on.

"Who do you think did this brickwork, Lynda?"

"Do you think it was artisans from the Vatican?"

"Thank God for the Baltimore Irish! Without them, none of this would be possible!"

By the time they reached the top, they were in tears from laughing so hard at their own absurdity.

A quintessential middle schooler, I was absolutely mortified by my parents. Becca and I distanced ourselves in the hopes that no one would see that we were with them.

Once Mom and Dad reached the top and got to the grotto itself, they saw the small stone amphitheater splayed out before them. They had been expecting some large, grand shrine, but all they discovered was another brick grotto the size of a large fireplace that housed some votive candles. They said, "What the heck is this? *This* is the Grotto of Our Lady of Lourdes?" There were maybe twenty or thirty people spread around the amphitheater, sitting quietly and praying, reading, or chatting.

Dad pushed Mom a little farther to investigate the grotto. Lo and behold, adjacent to the grotto was a metal bucket for people to put money in. And—you guessed it—the bucket had another bronze plaque. However, this time, instead of listing a Baltimore Irish family's name, the bronze plaque told a story:

The Vatican and the pope were so pleased and grateful for the work being done in eastern Maryland that as a token of their gratitude, the Vatican donated five hundred plenary indulgences to the Grotto of Our Lady of Lourdes.

At this point, my very Irish Catholic parents could no longer contain themselves.

For those who might not know, a plenary indulgence is, in the simplest of terms, a "get out of jail free" card. Did you cuss at your grandma? Cash in a plenary indulgence. Cheat on a test? Cash in a plenary indulgence. Did you murder someone? Make it rain plenary indulgences. And to have *five hundred* plenary indulgences donated from the pope himself? That, ladies and gents, was the plenary indulgence jackpot.

My parents were in hysterics by this point. As Mom sat in her wheelchair crying tears of laughter, my dad happened to notice a man behind them pointing at Mom and commenting to his wife, "Dolores, I think that woman over there is really experiencing something here . . . I think she's being healed!"

My dad, through stifled laughter, whispered to my mom, "Lynda, don't look now and don't laugh, but that man back there thinks you're being healed." A pregnant pause filled the air. Dad looked at her and nudged, "Lynda . . . you have to stand up."

My mom responded through her own laughter and tears, "No way. Absolutely not. Tom, there's no way. I'm not doing that."

"Lynda, you have to. You gotta stand up," he insisted.

"Tom, I can't . . ." She could barely breathe.

"Lynda, you gotta. Please. You have to. You must," Dad wheezed.

So, in the only way my mom knew how, she "yes and-ed" my dad and proceeded, for the next few moments, to dramatically rise from her wheelchair as though she were being healed. The drama! The suspense! The level at which she committed to this miraculous display of healing at the grotto was Oscar-worthy.

Everyone around them began to *ooh* and *ahh* and celebrate the miraculous healing they were fortunate enough to witness. There was applause! There was celebration! There were tears!

Meanwhile, from fifty yards away, Becca and I watched the whole thing go down. I could see my dad behind my mom, trying not to pee himself from laughing so hard. Then I looked at Becca and said, "Oh my gosh, they are so weird. Let's go find that holy water and pretend we don't know them."

When Mom finally sat back down, my parents walked up to the

stanchion and began to fill out a request form for a couple of plenary indulgences for their stunt.

After they calmed themselves and came back down to earth, they explored the grotto for a while and came upon the Saint Francis memorial. In a needed moment of solemnity, they sat and spent some time together praying and meditating. Despite their complicated relationships with their Catholic upbringings, the prayer of Saint Francis was something that meant a lot to both of my parents.

> *Lord, make me an instrument of your peace.*
> *Where there is hatred, let me sow love;*
> *where there is injury, pardon;*
> *where there is doubt, faith;*
> *where there is despair, hope;*
> *where there is darkness, light;*
> *and where there is sadness, joy.*
> *O Divine Master, grant that I may not so much seek to be*
>   *consoled as to console;*
> *to be understood as to understand;*
> *to be loved as to love.*
> *For it is in giving that we receive;*
> *it is in pardoning that we are pardoned;*
> *and it is in dying that we are born to eternal life.*
> *Amen.*

When it was time to head back to the motor home, my dad turned to my mom and said, "I have no idea where Molly and Becca went. But I sure hope they found some holy water."

Oh, Becca and I had found the holy water, all right. While my parents were off putting on the performance of a lifetime in front of an adoring crowd, Becca and I slipped away to avoid secondhand embarrassment. We had come around a corner to find the "holy water" fountain. I don't really know how to describe it other than as a stone fountain with holy water (from the Vatican!) with yet another bronze plaque donated by yet another Irish family from Baltimore. Becca and I had our pitchers in hand and did the only logical thing to do: put the holy water in the pitchers because this stuff was coming back with us! We were thirteen-year-old girls on a mission. We had big thirteen-year-old girl problems, and holy water was an obvious solution to them all. Quite proud of ourselves, Becca and I headed back to the motor home in the parking lot.

When my parents came down off the mountain, they discovered Becca and me in the motor home pouring holy water from our pitchers into small plastic spritzer bottles. Then we began spritzing said genuine Grotto of Our Lady of Lourdes holy water on our homework, our hair, our zits, and our boobs.

That was it. My parents were done. They laughed so hard they couldn't see straight. My dad was still wheezing. My mom was red in the face.

Becca and I couldn't figure out why they thought it was so funny. What else could we possibly use the holy water for?!

As objectionable as our humor might have been, the fact remained: Our family lived out the notion that "life is too short to take yourself too seriously." My parents knew that tomorrow with my mom wasn't promised. Her life was a ticking clock. Therefore, we would be a family who laughed and found joy in even the bleakest of situations. I'm so thankful to have had parents who showed me what it looked like to laugh hard, work hard, and love harder. We had PhDs in living in the tension of the joy and the grief.

Heaven only knew how much we would need and cling to that laughter in the days, weeks, months, and years to come.

9

DOUBTING THOMAS

1985–2003

> When I was a kid, I used to pray every night for a new
> bike. Then I realised, the Lord doesn't work that way.
> So I just stole one and asked Him to forgive me.

EMO PHILIPS

Unlike my parents, I didn't grow up in church. My parents had wrestled greatly over whether to raise me in some kind of faith tradition, but for better or for worse, they ultimately decided not to force any kind of religion on me and let me figure it out along the way. For my parents, the hurt they'd experienced in church growing up (often literally hurt, seeing as they'd been paddled regularly by nuns in school) left them somewhat disillusioned. But that also meant their "Catholic guilt" wouldn't allow them to *not* give me a godmother or *not* have me christened, so I was christened in the living room of our home a few months after I was born.

For my parents, the fellowship and traditions of Alcoholics Anonymous became their faith community. AA was their church. Meetings (two, three, five nights a week) were their gathering of believers. AA was founded by Christians, and everything from the twelve steps to the twelve traditions to the "Big Book" to the recitation of the Serenity Prayer and Lord's Prayer at the end of meetings were all founded on Christian principles. AA was where my parents found each other, where they found faith again, where they met God again, and where they found wholeness.

As a kid, I would go with my parents to AA meetings all the time—sometimes three or four days a week. This wasn't strange at all. Most AA meetings met in churches, and I would either sit in on the meeting and quietly color or find a random Sunday school classroom down the hall to play in.

When I was about five years old, my parents came in my room to find me sitting on the floor in a circle with my Barbies and stuffed animals. I was facilitating an AA meeting.

"Whatcha doin', Molly?" Mom asked curiously.

"Mom! Ken fell off the Radio Flyer wagon. Barbie picked him up and brought him to this meeting, and she's making him accept his shortcomings. Oh, and Bear is about to pick up his thirty-day chip!"

Simulating the meeting

"Hi, I'm Bear, and I'm an alcoholic. And today I've been sober thirty days!"

"Hiiiiii, Bear!" the rest of the animals replied in unison.

My parents walked out of the room unable to contain their laughter, while simultaneously realizing they *might* need to find a sitter for when they went to AA meetings from there on out.

I knew a lot about alcoholics and a little about Jesus. If I even *saw* someone drinking a beer or holding a glass of wine, I'd automatically assume they were an alcoholic. All I knew of Jesus was that he had long, flowy hair like Mel Gibson (this was the late '80s, after all), he wore a white robe with a purple sash, and a bunch of pictures of him nailed to a cross were hung around the church. That was it.

It was also around that same age when I consciously remember going to one of my first Catholic masses. I'd gone with my aunt and cousins and remember being so confused by all the sitting down, standing up, sitting down again, kneeling on the kneeler thing, more standing up, different hand gestures, thumb gestures, singing in a language I didn't understand, and random bells chiming off in the distance. Where *were* those bells coming from?! I was really confused.

But then, toward the end of the service, everyone in the sanctuary stood up for the recitation of the Lord's Prayer. I stood, *again*, and held hands with the stranger standing next to me, a woman whose palms were unbelievably clammy. I was barely four feet tall, but I was so excited because—finally! Something I knew!

I recited that Lord's Prayer with gusto! And confidence! A smile stretched across my tiny, freckled face as I said aloud with pride:

> *Our Father!*
> *Who art in heaven!*
> *Hallowed be thy name!*
> *Thy kingdom come!*
> *Thy will be done!*
> *On earth as it is in heaven!*
> *Give us this day our daily bread!*
> *And forgive us our trespasses!*
> *As we forgive those who trespass against us!*
> *And lead us not into temptation!*
> *But deliver us from evil!*

Now, I was unaware that for Catholics the Lord's Prayer ended at this point—and I was too lost and caught up in the moment, and my confidence was way too high, for me to pay attention to the fact that everyone else had ceased speaking.

So I did as the folks in AA do and continued on . . .

> *For thine is the kingdom!*
> *And the power!*
> *And the glory!*
> *Forever and ever and ever and ever!*
> *Amen!*

At this point in the Lord's Prayer, even the *non-Catholics* stop talking. But not the alcoholics! They keep going!

I shook that clammy stranger's hand up and down as I concluded with a hearty:

> *Keep coming back! It works if you work it!*

The large, ornate sanctuary was otherwise silent, but my five-year-old voice ricocheted off every post, ceiling beam, and piece of stained glass in the building.

It is not even close to an exaggeration when I say that every eyeball in the place was fixed on me. The tall lady with the clammy hand to my left let go of me with fervor, so as not to appear as though she was with me. I had no idea what had just happened, so I proceeded to slowly sit down and wonder why everyone was staring at me. I did it right! *Right?*

I heard someone a few rows back stifling laughter. The priest cleared his throat and moved on to the next part of the service.

"Lord Jesus Christ,

who said to your Apostles,

'Peace I leave you, my peace I give you . . .'"

It would be years before I'd enter a Catholic church again.

———

My next real introduction to Christianity was in elementary school through my best friend Lisa. Lisa and I became friends in the second grade, and we were inseparable. We went to each other's houses all the time after school, we'd have sleepovers and stay up late playing Mall Madness and Dream Phone, and we'd travel with each other on family trips. Lisa was the best. She was so kind to me amid some of the bullying I experienced, and I thought we were going to be friends forever. We'd talk about being in each other's weddings and raising our kids together so they could be best friends too.

Lisa came from a really strong Christian family. Her parents always prayed before dinner and would read a devotional to us before bed whenever I spent the night. One night, Lisa's mom said, "Lisa, why don't you invite Molly with us to Awana next week? I think she'd really enjoy it!"

The next thing I knew, I was going to Awana. Now, I had no idea what Awana was, but what I *did* know was that I got to wear a vest like my Girl Scout vest and got to earn patches like my Girl Scout patches. Did I know what those patches were for? Absolutely not. But since I thrived on tangible tokens of achievement, I was going to do whatever a grown-up told me to do in order to earn them.

I vividly remember memorizing John 3:16 just so I could earn a patch: "For God so loved the world, that he gave his only begotten Son, that whosoever believeth in him should not perish, but have everlasting life" (KJV).

Did I have a clue what that verse meant? Once again, no. But I got a patch! My Awana attendance was sporadic at best, but I'd go anytime Lisa invited me because I loved patches and loved my friend Lisa.

A few years went by, and one day in the fifth grade, Lisa came up to me during PE. It was raining that day, so we were in the gym playing popcorn with the best bouncy balls and the biggest rainbow parachute. (Any '90s kid knows this was the best kind of PE day.)

"Hi, Molly, can I talk to you?" Lisa asked.

"Sure, Lisa!" I said excitedly.

Lisa grabbed my hand. Then she pulled me away from the parachute and into a small room right off the gym. We sat down on the cold linoleum floor, surrounded by "Got Milk?" and Successories motivational posters taped to the cinder block walls.

"Molly, we can't be friends anymore," she said bluntly.

"Wait, huh? What do you mean?" I asked.

"We have to stop being friends. I don't want to be your friend anymore. We won't be friends after this," she coldly replied.

I sat still for a moment, staring just over Lisa's shoulder at Joan Lunden. Joan sat power-posed in a red blazer, sporting a milk mustache and staring right back at me. Underneath Joan read the words: "MILK: What a Surprise!" Next to Joan was another poster that said "TEAMWORK," featuring a bunch of guys in a rowboat.

The irony.

I began to tear up. "What? Why? Why can't we be friends anymore, Lisa?"

"You're not Christian enough for me, Molly." This is a direct quote. Lisa stood up and walked out of the room. I watched her walk away and then pick up a piece of the parachute.

I was stunned. I didn't know what to do, so I sat there and began to cry. I felt so hurt, devastated, and alone. Lisa and I did everything together! What did she mean I wasn't "Christian" enough for her? Did I not go to Awana enough? Did I not earn enough patches? Was this because I told her that her parents were alcoholics because I saw beer in their fridge?

If this was what being "Christian" was about, I wanted nothing to do with the church.

My parents never discouraged me from going to church; they allowed me to search however I saw fit. But one Sunday when I was about ten years old, my mom came in my room, woke me up, and said, "Get dressed in something nice. You're coming with me." Truth be told, I don't remember where my dad was that day—probably out playing golf—so it was just me and Mom. I got dressed and came downstairs, and she said, "Let's go."

We got in the car and drove for about ten minutes until we turned off the main road and onto a narrow gravel road lined with large oak trees. "Where are we going, Mom?" I asked.

"You'll see," she winked as she replied with a mischievous grin on her face, like some secret awaited us.

I hadn't seen her like this in a long time, if ever.

At the end of the gravel road, we approached a little white church with a beautiful wooden cross on top. I heard loud music playing and saw people pouring into the church.

"What are we doing here?" I asked.

"What do you think? We're going to church," she said.

"What church is this?"

"A fun one," she replied confidently.

Mom grabbed her crutches, then handed me her purse and her jug of Diet Coke. She gestured for me to follow her as we walked up the steps into the church. It took absolutely zero time for me to realize we were at an all-Black church. The clapping, the dancing, the music, and the gospel choir could likely be heard for miles.

Despite our attempts to "slip in," a fortysomething white lady with crutches and too many personal belongings and a ten-year-old girl in a green velvet American Girl replica dress (Samantha's) absolutely stuck out like a sore thumb in a small Black church.

I was very confused why I'd been brought to this place with zero context.

I stood next to Mom, who smiled and clapped and bobbed her head with the choir, singing, "I have decided to follow Jesus, no turnin' back, no turnin' back!"

The music went on for what felt like hours, and Mom loved every second of it. I listened as the pastor got up and preached his heart out, not having a clue as to what he was saying. Mom's gaze was fixed on the pastor, her eyes watery, the edges of her mouth upturned like she was about to smile.

He finished preaching, the choir got back up, they sang a few more hymns, and the service ended. A few people thanked us for being there, and my mom did what only my mom could do: make friends with everyone she spoke to. She beamed. I said nothing.

We left the building and got in the car, and Mom sighed heavily, exclaiming, "Oh, I loved that."

Then we went home, not speaking another word about it.

Over the next couple of years, she did that very same thing a few more times. She would wake me up on a Sunday, get me dressed, and take me to that little Black church down the road. She'd smile and sing and hug, and then we'd leave. Occasionally I'd look over just as a tear streamed down her cheek. I never knew why we made those Sunday trips, and I never asked. That was that.

As an adult, I've thought a lot about those Sunday mornings. I hate to say I have regrets, but I deeply regret not asking more questions. Honestly, I regret not asking my mom more questions, period. But something about those Sundays was different.

My mom's relationship with the big-*C* Church was complicated—as we know, a strict upbringing can have that effect—but I always knew my mom believed in God and had a personal relationship with Jesus. I simply think she didn't know how to convey that. Those Sunday mornings were times when she could go to a place with no pretenses, no facades, and no chances of having to say a dozen Hail Marys. She knew she could let loose there and be in the presence of God.

And in some ways, I think it was her way of saying without saying, "See, Molly, this is what church is about."

Also, she loved gospel music, so that probably didn't hurt.

In middle school, I met Lillian. We were in chorus together, and Lillian could sing. Like, *sing* sing. She was so good. Middle school was where I really began to grow in confidence in my own singing, and Lillian played a huge part in that. Lillian also came from a strong Christian family, and I'd be lying to you if I said I wasn't hesitant to become friends with her because of that. But since we hit it off, I got over that very quickly.

By our freshman year of high school, Lillian and I were really close. We were in all the choirs together and hung out a ton after school. She'd invited me to church a few times, and I went with her once but was so uncomfortable I'd made excuses every other time she'd asked. One day during some downtime in chorus, Lillian came up to me and said, "Hey, Molly! Some friends and I have started a Christian worship band, and we need another singer. Would you be interested in joining me as a co-lead singer?"

What? Me? Co-lead singer in a band? *A Christian worship band?*

"I mean, that would be really cool, but you know I don't really go to church," I told her.

"That's okay," she said. "You can sing and help lead the songs. You'll learn! Why don't you join us for a band practice?"

"Okay, I'll come check it out."

I went to her friend David's house for our first practice. David, the drummer, was a junior in high school, and he was amazing. Steven was our guitarist, also a junior, and Nathan was our bass player.

We called ourselves Doubting Thomas.

I was shocked at how much I loved being a part of Doubting Thomas. Being in a band was so fun, and I actually loved the music. We started to "travel" and play youth group nights at local churches. In my mind we were famous, full-time touring musicians when, in reality, we played about five gigs, tops.

Our set list included smash hits like:

"Heart of Worship"
"Lord, I Lift Your Name on High"
"Better Is One Day"
"Shout to the Lord"
"Shine, Jesus, Shine"
"I Could Sing of Your Love Forever"

And we always closed out the set with the clubhouse favorite, "Sanctuary" (sung in a round, of course).

I don't really know what happened to Doubting Thomas. Like a lot of things, it just sort of fizzled out. One day we stopped rehearsing, and churches stopped asking us to come play.

Lillian and I stayed friends, but I never went to church with her again—and, like Doubting Thomas, we eventually grew apart too.

Later on in high school, I occasionally joined my friend Katie for Sunday Mass at Saint Joseph Catholic Church. I went solely for the purpose of seeing Mike, a guy from my golf team, because I had a huge crush on him and hoped maybe he'd reciprocate if he saw me as a good Catholic girl.

Lord, forgive me, for I knew not what I was doing.

For those early years of my life, I was fumbling around in the dark looking for a light switch when it came to my relationship with God. I associated faith with rules, and I'd been told I wasn't "this enough" or "that enough." Ironically, I was not all that different from the actual Doubting Thomas who needed a real, close, personal encounter with Jesus in order to believe. I spent years doubting God, even making fun of Christians at times, thinking there was no way that a kind, loving God would let bad things happen to good people.

The truth is, I had no firm foundation on which to place anything in my life. Everything I did was in pursuit of what "looked good" or what would earn me praise from others. I was desperate for acceptance. I was desperate to be successful. I was desperate to be liked and loved and popular. I was desperate to believe I was in control of my own destiny. I was building a proverbial house on sinking sand. So when the storm came and the winds blew—and they were coming—any semblance of faith I had would topple right along with it.

MAKING FRIENDS

Twenty years since my life was changed
Twenty years making a friend of death
Knowing it
Respecting it
Wishing for it at times
Fighting with it as friends sometimes do.
But the nightmares of war have faded as I've healed
My dreams are now of peace
Peace of mind
Peace of heart
Hoping for Peace on earth
It's time I made a friend of Life.

—LYNDA VAN DEVANTER BUCKLEY,
VISIONS OF WAR, DREAMS OF PEACE

10

MAKING FRIENDS

NOVEMBER 15, 2002

If today were the last day of my life, would I
want to do what I am about to do today?

STEVE JOBS

Most teenagers spend the majority of their school years anticipating
the start of their senior year of high school. It's about standing at the
threshold of real life, filled with reflection and anticipation. It's a place
where we realize that all roads led to this moment, every past memory
is woven into our stories, and a bright future with endless possibilities
awaits us. For me, it was no different, but with Mom's illness, there
was always a cloud that hung over our family.

In the fall of my senior year, I'd begun hanging out with a boy
named James from my Spanish class. We'd gone to my senior home-
coming together and a couple of group dates, and things were getting
pretty serious.

One cool Sunday night in mid-November, he had come over to
my house to visit. When it was time for him to go, I walked him out
to his car and he leaned in and kissed me against his turquoise 1995

Toyota Corolla. With his arms around my waist, he leaned back a little and looked me in the eye and asked me to officially be his girlfriend. To which I played it very cool and said, "Yes!" as he kissed me again. I was so deeply in puppy love, I could barely contain myself.

After I watched him pull out of the driveway, I frolicked back into the house to find my mom and dad on the couch watching *Alias*. The grin of a Cheshire cat was plastered across my face.

"You have a boyfriend now, huh," Mom stated.

Seventeen-year-old me could do nothing but giggle and squeal.

"He's a sweet kid, honey. I'm very happy for you," she continued.

Dad, being very much a dad, kept his eyes locked on Sydney Bristow and said nothing.

Dad was supposed to be leaving the next day for a two-week training for golf teaching professionals in Las Vegas, so the subject was quickly changed from new boyfriends to doctor's appointments, medication schedules, and other things I'd need to know for the week ahead.

Mom's health had taken a rough turn, and my dad was having a hard time leaving for his trip. The Molotov cocktail of medications du jour that my mom was on made her loopy and borderline incoherent at times. Additionally, this particular combination of meds prohibited her from driving herself anywhere, which meant I'd need to play chauffeur and run any necessary errands.

"I feel like I should stay, Lynda. There's always next year for this training," said Dad.

"Don't be ridiculous, Tom. You've been preparing for and looking forward to this training for months. I'm fine! We will be fine! Go. We've got this. You don't give us nearly enough credit," she joked.

Dad surrendered. "Fine. But you know how to reach me if you need me."

Dad left Monday morning, and I headed off to school. Throughout the week I'd call home from school to check in with Mom during the day, only to find her watching her soap operas or waking up from a nap.

Dad would also call regularly to check in to see how things were going. From the moment he'd left for Vegas, he was uneasy and couldn't relax. By Thursday, he had this sinking feeling he needed to come home. He later described it to me as this "incredible pull"—this pure connection with my mom that told him he needed to be home. Dad went to the training coordinator and said, "I'm so sorry, this isn't feeling right to me. I can come back, but I have to get home. I will have to do this training next year."

He dropped everything, went back to his hotel room, packed up, and headed to the airport to catch the first flight home.

"Dad, why are you coming home early? Do you not trust me?" I asked when he called that afternoon to tell me his plans.

"I feel uneasy, Molly. Don't argue with me about this. I'm coming home." He wouldn't relent.

NOVEMBER 14, 2002

Dad wasn't home yet, so I called to check on Mom. She didn't answer the home phone, but when I tried her cell phone, she answered. I could tell right away she wasn't at home. I could hear noise in the background that was characteristic of the grocery store.

"Mom! Are you out?!" I exclaimed.

"I just had to run a couple of quick errands, honey. I needed more ChapStick and shampoo from the drugstore, and then I realized we were almost out of milk, raisins, and All-Bran, so I—"

I cut her off yelling, "Mom! You cannot do that! You know you're not supposed to be driving. You are to call me or wait for me to get home. Mom, this is dangerous. Stay where you are. I'll talk to the school secretary and tell her what's going on, and then I will come to get you."

"Molly, no. You will not do that. I'm going to finish my errands and then go straight home. I am just fine and perfectly capable of driving myself," she argued.

"Mom, no!"

She hung up.

I was furious. She knew better. She could have hurt herself or someone else. I didn't know what to do. I was convinced I knew what was best, but I was too mad to do anything at that moment. I also knew Mom was too stubborn to listen to me, so I went back to class and tried to calm myself down.

The reality was, I was too immature to put myself in my mom's shoes. I was a typical, narrow-minded teenager who got frustrated by her parents and I struggled to see them for who they were: independent, whole humans who had a life and experiences and dreams and hardships outside of parenting me. Especially my mom. Our particularly unique set of circumstances led me to a position where I thought I knew better than her. I was right and she was wrong.

When I got home from school that afternoon, I stormed into the house. I slammed the door and didn't take a moment to breathe before I began castigating my mom for her behavior.

"How could you do this, Mom?!" I yelled.

"Molly, do not speak to me this way," she said firmly.

"Mom! I wouldn't have to if you'd just listened to everyone around you! If you don't listen to me, listen to your doctors! I feel like we constantly have to remind you that no matter what you think, you just can't do certain things. It's not safe!"

I yelled and she yelled and we yelled.

The years of grief, fear, pent-up frustration, anger, and resentment toward a stupid illness began to pour out of us through the words we hurled at each other. Worry, stress, anxiety, and fatigue lurked beneath the surface of it all. I don't think it was even about the driving anymore; it was the culmination of eight years of big feelings that had nowhere else to go. I said awful things I wanted to take back almost immediately.

It all ended with me storming upstairs and slamming the door to my attic bedroom. Which, because the house was so old, didn't really even close, let alone slam. But I was bound and determined to be as dramatic as possible.

Silence.

My dad came home and immediately felt the thick tension in the air.

That evening we had dinner, and my dad left to go to an AA meeting. I called my boyfriend. I watched television. I avoided Mom. After Dad got home from his meeting, he went upstairs and lay in bed with my mom, snuggling and talking. He treasured those moments together because he knew in his heart they didn't have many of those nights left.

After talking for a while, he got up, said good night, and went to bed in the guest room. It was nearly eleven p.m. when I decided to go to bed. I'd said hardly any words to my mother between the time we'd ended our argument and when I decided it was time to end the day. I was walking back upstairs from getting a glass of water and passed the door to my mom's room. Her door was open, and she was sitting in the middle of her bed reading. I wasn't going to speak to her, but she stopped me on my way to my room.

"Molly."

I stood in the doorway to her room, staring at her. A pregnant moment of silence hung in the air between us. So much said, but even more left unsaid.

"Molly, sweetheart, I love you."

Her eyes were fixed on me.

The moment when we made eye contact is one of the most vivid memories I have.

Her eyes had this haunting look to them, the blues of her irises bluer than ever before—so blue I could see it from the doorway. And yet, there was a haze on them . . . a strange glassiness I couldn't shake.

I stared back at her.

"I love you, too, Mom." If the rolling of eyes can have a tone of voice, that is how I said those words.

And I closed my door, went upstairs, and went to sleep.

NOVEMBER 15, 2002, 1:30 A.M.

Something began to shake me. I was dreaming.

"Molly.

"Molly."

The voice was no louder than a whisper, but the words were clear.

"Molly.

"Molly.

"Molly."

I opened my eyes. It was pitch-black, but I could see the whites of my dad's eyes piercing through the darkness.

His hand on my arm as he sat on the end of my bed and shook me, his voice shaking.

"Molly."

I knew.

The tears in his voice as he continued, "Molly. It's your . . ."

I sat bolt upright in bed.

"No, Dad. No. No. No. No. No. No!"

"It's your mom, honey. I found her—"

"Dad. Stop! No!"

I got up and began to run downstairs.

"Molly, don't!" he cried. "Don't go. Don't go in there. I don't want you to see her," Dad said firmly, yet still never above a whisper.

Everything moved in slow motion as I ran down the stairs of my room and rounded the corner. I ran into my parents' bathroom and stopped.

There she was. My mother. My amazing, strong, stubborn, incredible mother. My image of her at that moment is forever etched into every crevice of my brain, but too tender for me to ever articulate.

I fell to the floor screaming.

"No, Mom! No. Dad, no! This isn't happening. This isn't real. Dad, call 911!"

"I already have, sweetheart. Your mom is gone."

"No, Dad! She's not gone!" I wailed, *"Do something!* Call 911! Get them here!"

"They're on the way, honey. They are. There's nothing they can do. She's gone, sweetheart. She's gone. I'm so sorry. She's gone."

Tears streamed down his cheeks as I screamed. A guttural, primal sound that emanated from the depths of my soul. I began to slap myself violently, thinking that if I slapped myself hard enough, I'd wake up from the nightmare.

This wasn't happening.

"Mom, I'm so sorry. I'm so sorry, Mom. I love you, Mom. Come back, please. God, please! Please bring her back, God. If you really exist, God, bring her back. I'm begging you." I repeated these in some form over and over again.

I sat there on the floor of the bathroom staring at her in stunned silence.

I watched as Dad hugged her lifeless body. "Your job is done," he whispered in her ear, "and you did one hell of a job."

Moments later, I heard the faint sound of sirens approaching. The same paramedic unit had been to our home in the middle of the night previously, so I recognized their faces. Yet this time, their faces wore much different expressions.

The paramedics started interviewing my dad, asking him question after question. They all sounded like the adults on *Peanuts* to me: "*Wom wom wom wom wom.*"

I couldn't take my eyes off my mother. I was no longer screaming. The tears had stopped as I went numb.

Dad was trying to get ahold of Mom's doctor, Dr. Reynolds, to connect him with the paramedics so they could identify a cause of death.

I continued to stare at her and listen to the conversations around me.

"Respiratory illness."

"Vital signs?"

"Suffocation?"

"Was CPR administered?"

"Pulmonary edema."

"Cause of death?"

A female paramedic put her hand on my shoulder and said to me, "Sweetheart, I think you should leave while we do what we need to do. Why don't you go downstairs and call someone?"

In a daze, I walked out of the bathroom, and on the wall right outside was a framed, cross-stitched version of the Serenity Prayer.

God, grant me the serenity
to accept the things I cannot change,
the courage to change the things I can,
and the wisdom to know the difference.
Amen.

I stared at it as I had done a thousand times before. Yet, suddenly, the meaning of it felt so much heavier.

I went downstairs and sat on the couch in the living room, wondering what to do next. I picked up the phone and called my new boyfriend of five whole days and somehow, someway, he answered.

With almost no emotion in my voice, I said, "My mom is dead. I need you to come over." What else do you say when you call someone under those circumstances?

Twenty minutes later, he was there.

I called a few of my best friends, Rachel, Sarah, Katie, Staci, and Becca. Katie was away at her boyfriend's graduation from marine boot camp, but Sarah's mom answered the phone. Staci answered the phone. My uncle, Steve, also answered the phone.

"My mom is dead. I need you."

Within thirty minutes, they were all there.

We all sat in the quiet living room. I stared straight ahead, my gaze fixed on absolutely nothing. The sounds of the voices of the paramedics upstairs. My dad on the phone. I sat in silence. My friends and boyfriend talking with each other. Everyone crying. Everyone stunned.

Time stood still, and time flew. Time was this thing that was no longer relevant to my life. I had no concept of what day of the week it was, what year we were in, or what I would do next. Everything came to a halt.

What felt like hours later, the paramedics came and told us to move into the dining room so they could bring down my mother's body on the gurney.

We walked into the dining room, and I stood for a moment and thought, *No! I need to see her one more time.*

The paramedics stopped in the foyer. Her body lay in a body bag on the stretcher. I looked the paramedic in the eye and said, "Please, I need to see her one more time."

They unzipped the bag, and I brought my hand to her face. I kissed her on the temple and whispered, "I love you, too, Mom. I love you. I love you. I'm so sorry."

I'd said the same words to her hours earlier with teenage sass and attitude. This time I spoke with every last ounce of love and emotion I could muster, hoping I'd somehow make it up to her.

Then out the door they went. As the door shut, so did I.

One by one, my friends, my boyfriend, and my uncle left our house, leaving my dad and me in silence.

I wasn't going back to sleep, so I sat there.

My dad tried desperately to get ahold of my sister, but she was on a cruise at the time and unreachable. For the next few hours, I sat and said nothing as I listened to him make phone calls.

At about six a.m., I had the bright idea that I should go to school. I took a shower, got dressed, and got in the car. I didn't have my backpack or any of my books, but I drove to school anyway. I pulled into my parking space, got out of the car, and walked into the building.

My eyes never looked to the left or right, only straight ahead. I was a zombie.

I didn't have the faintest clue where I was going, but the senior assistant principal immediately stopped me in the hallway. He took me by the shoulders and led me into his office.

I said nothing.

"Molly, what on earth are you doing here? Sarah's mom called me and told me what happened. Why are you here?" He was incredulous.

"Because it's a school day and I have to go to school."

"Okay, well, where's your backpack?"

"At home."

"Are your books in your locker?"

"No."

"What's your first class this morning?"

"I don't know."

"Molly, go home."

"Okay . . . will you tell my teachers for me? I don't want to get an unexcused absence. What about my homework? Will you have them send me my homework? What if I fall behind? I can be back on Monday."

"Molly, go home."

He ushered me out the door, and I walked back to my car only to find it still running in the parking lot.

So I did what I had to: I got in the car and drove home.

11

TWENTY-ONE DOVES

NOVEMBER 20, 2002

[Funerals.] Amazing tradition. They throw a great party
for you on the one day they know you can't come.

JEFF GOLDBLUM IN *THE BIG CHILL*

Death is the most unavoidable part of life. You're born. You live. You
die. Guaranteed. And yet it's a part of life that so many of us do nothing but fear. For years I heard that public speaking is the only thing
people fear more than death, but I was curious about the current sta-
tistics. Then I discovered a 2021 survey done by Chapman University
on the top ten self-reported fears for Americans. To my surprise, public
speaking was not even on the list. What *was* in the top ten?

10. 49.3 percent of respondents feared biological warfare. *This is
    reasonable, as it would more than likely kill you or someone you
    love.*
9. 50.8 percent feared the pollution of oceans, rivers, and lakes.
   *Pollution kills animals and stuff, and I guess it can kill us too. It
   should be noted that this fear ranked #2 in 2019.*

8. 51 percent feared cyber-terrorism. *I think, somehow, this could kill us?*

7. 54.8 percent feared economic collapse. *Not directly related to death, but . . .*

6. 55.8 percent feared a pandemic or major epidemic. *Yet another thing that would likely kill us or the people we love. Gee, I wonder where this fear came from?*

5. 56.5 percent feared widespread civil unrest. *This list gets better and better.*

4. 57.3 percent feared the people they loved would become seriously ill. *From a pandemic? Or water pollution? Or biological warfare? Or just in general? Or civil unrest?*

3. 58 percent feared a loved one would contract the coronavirus (COVID-19). *Well, we didn't have coronavirus on our 2019 bingo card when this survey was previously done, did we?*

2. 58.5 percent feared the death of loved ones. *Wait, didn't we just admit to this in at least six of the previous fears?*

And the number one fear that Americans had in 2021?

1. 79.6 percent feared corrupt government officials.[*]

It could be easily argued that eight out of the top ten fears Americans have are related to death and dying—especially concerning our loved ones. I cannot get over the fact that the only thing we fear *more* than that is the corruption of our government officials. We are unwell. *Jesus, come get us.*

So now that we've cleared all that up . . . *why* do we fear death so much? Haven't we, since birth, been surrounded by people we knew

---

[*] For more on this survey, visit https://www.chapman.edu/wilkinson/research-centers /babbie-center/_files/Babbie%20center%20fear2021/blogpost-americas-top-fears-2020 _-21-final.pdf.

would die? And why do we tend to handle death and grief so poorly in our culture? I don't have the stats, theories, or hypotheses to back any of these thoughts up, as I am not a psychologist, and this isn't a book about the fear of death. I ask these rhetorical questions because even after all of the death I've experienced in my life, I don't really have a great answer.

My parents had been mentally, emotionally, and spiritually preparing for my mother's death for eight years. Her original prognosis had been "two years, at best." She got eight. In many ways, my dad had slowly grieved the death of his beloved over the course of time. However, while I'd known she was sick and that the disease would "take her eventually," I was completely unaware that her death was imminent and each day she woke up with breath in her lungs was a gift. So while Dad was prepared, I was not. For me, Mom's death was sudden and unexpected, and at the age of seventeen, I was in no way equipped with any sort of emotional or spiritual tools to cope with it.

Everything between the night Mom died and the day of her funeral was a blur. The days all blended together. I slept erratically; I ate sparingly. I didn't cry. I was numb. Our house had historically been full of people, and this moment was certainly no exception. Our home was a revolving door of my friends, kids from school, teachers, my parents' friends, AA people, town council members, veterans, and neighbors. Everyone brought a country ham (*so many country hams*). Casseroles and lasagnas. Flower arrangements and plants. We sifted through thousands of emails and letters of condolence. Hundreds of care packages were sent to the house. Random women would walk in and start vacuuming. Somehow my laundry was done and folded and placed on my dresser. My sheets were changed, and my bed was made. I remember going into the bathroom one day, and someone had taken the time to fold the top layer of toilet paper into a little triangle . . . you know, like they do in hotel rooms. I remember thinking, *How on earth is a folded piece of toilet paper that I'm going to wipe my butt with supposed to make me feel better about my mother's death?*

While Dad had made every attempt to get in touch with Bridgid, he was finally able to reach her friend Jen, who was going to pick Bridgid up at the airport. When Jen picked her up, she told Bridgid the horrible news, took her home to unpack and repack her suitcase, and got her on the road to Herndon. When she got to our house, my friend Becca was in my room with me, and Bridgid said nothing but just crawled into bed with me and we cried.

My brand-spankin'-new boyfriend James brought me flowers or a Wendy's Frosty nearly every day. He'd sit with me and try to make me laugh while we channel surfed or listened to music. There was a flurry of activity around me, but all I could do was sit and watch it go by.

My mom's friend Jennie, who happened to be her ex-husband Bill's sister (I know—odd, right?), came to town to help us with the funeral logistics. There was so much to think about:

The date of the service
The location of the service
The time of the service
The order of the service
Would there be a viewing or not?
Would we have multiple viewings?
What songs would be sung?
Who would speak?
Where would she be buried?

We need to write an obituary . . .

Oh, we need to get a casket too . . .

Someone needs to contact the VA so we can get her full military
     honors . . .

How on earth are we going to pull off releasing twenty-one
     doves?

Can we eat all the country hams at the reception after the
     service?

How can we politely tell people to stop bringing country hams?

The list went on.

Mom was not one for fanfare or notoriety, and she likely would
have cringed at the notion of her obit being published in a major
newspaper. But Jennie wasn't having it. "Lynda impacted people," she
said, "and people need to know she's passed." Jennie was able to get
the obituary written and featured in the *New York Times*, *Time*, the
Washington Post, the *Los Angeles Times*, the *San Francisco Chronicle*,
and of course, the *Herndon Observer*.

My dad, Bridgid, and I went down to Adams-Green, the tiny
funeral home in downtown Herndon, to meet with the funeral director. We sat there, none of us crying . . . we were all going through the
motions in a clinical way. Step by step. One thing at a time.

Something we determined early on was that the funeral home was
not nearly large enough for the service, so we opted for two visitation
time slots at Adams-Green, a funeral the next day at Saint Timothy's
Episcopal Church down the road, and another graveside service to
follow.

After we made that decision, the funeral director looked at us and
said, "Okay, the next step is to pick out the casket. Follow me."

Wait a second . . . We have to pick out *a casket? This isn't like a standard thing that is chosen for you? It's a box that goes into the ground; why does it matter? Why is this something we have to decide on, like a new set of drapes?* I was flummoxed, but I was also woefully unprepared for what would come next.

The funeral director ushered us down the hallway in this old home that was the funeral parlor. Then he opened up a door that led to a small room . . . full of caskets.

I immediately screamed. I wailed.

Until this moment, I hadn't cried since shortly after the paramedics left the previous Friday. I'd held in all of my emotions through every country ham delivery and folded toilet paper roll. The room of caskets was just too much for me. I couldn't even step inside.

To this day, I still don't know why that sight was so jarring, but I couldn't function. It was, by far, the hardest part of the funeral planning process for me. I became undone. My dad lost it, my sister lost it, and I was a complete wreck. The funeral director tried to speak words of reassurance, but I was having absolutely none of it.

"You're paid to say that! You don't mean any of that! You deal with this all the time!"

I was destroyed.

I have no idea how long it took me to get myself together. It could have been eight minutes; it could have been three hours. I have no clue. I eventually calmed myself down enough to be able to walk into the room.

The room was only about twenty feet by twenty feet, and I walked around the open caskets like a maze. Each had different features, colors, hardware, and linings. I still couldn't believe this was something we had to decide on. This was a box we would put the body of my mother in! It wasn't fair.

We left the funeral home and walked across the street to my

favorite Mexican restaurant, the Tortilla Factory.[†] I ordered up a massive, sizzling plate of fajitas[‡] and put back about four baskets of chips and salsa.

Back at home, Dad, Bridgid, Jennie, and I sat down at the computer to draft the program for the service. We knew we wanted it to be a true celebration and tribute to her life, so we just hoped (and prayed) we could do her even a little bit of justice.

We'd contacted the VA, and they were arranging for the full military honors.

"I see here on Mrs. Buckley's file that she doesn't want the twenty-one-gun salute?"

"That's correct," Dad replied.

"Are you sure?"

"No guns. Only doves," Dad insisted.

"We can't provide doves, Mr. Buckley."

"I know; we will find a way," he said.

After calling around, we were able to locate a dove guy. That was his whole thing: he had doves he would bring to weddings to release. We lined up her pallbearers—friends in AA, her cousin, her brother-in-law, women she served with in Vietnam, and Dr. Reynolds, her respiratory pulmonologist. (Doesn't everyone have their pulmonologist serving as their pallbearer?) We also got an honor guard that consisted of six men who were part of a Vietnam veteran PTSD therapy group in DC. Mom was the only woman allowed to "call in," and they treated her like one of their own. Lastly, I asked two of my band friends from

---

† Fun fact, the Tortilla Factory was, and still is to this very day, my favorite restaurant of all time. We ate there every week growing up since it was walking distance from our house. One summer, I proudly ate there seventy-six days in a row. The Tortilla Factory closed in 2012, and I still haven't recovered. May it rest in peace.

‡ For the Gen Z folks reading this, ordering fajitas was a way to garner attention in the days before social media.

school, Drew and Andrew, if they would play taps on their trumpets at the conclusion of the graveside service, and they generously accepted.

———

The service was planned for Wednesday, and the visitations would take place the day before. We arrived at the funeral home about thirty minutes before the first visitation began. When I walked in the door and caught a glimpse of the open casket in the back room, I froze. I knew I couldn't go back there. I stood in the front room of the funeral home and wouldn't budge. Slowly but surely, people began to arrive for the visitation, and soon we found ourselves with a receiving line nearly three hours long. I couldn't believe how many people had traveled from all over the country to be there to pay their respects, to say goodbye, and to offer us their condolences in person.

By the night's end, everyone had left and the place was quiet. I silently stood there, staring into the abyss of paisley wallpaper and brocade Windsor chairs, processing the events of the evening. Dad gestured that it was time to go, but I had not yet ventured into the back room. I knew this was my last chance to see her face and say goodbye, so I moved toward where she lay in the open casket.

I crept up to the casket and collapsed. There was something so permanent about seeing her lying there. I stood and placed my hand on her cheek while tears streamed down my own. "I love you, Mom. I love you. I'm so sorry. I love you."

The funeral director placed his hands on my shoulders, gestured toward the door, and said it was time to go. It was incredibly late and way past the time the last visitation was supposed to end. I watched as he slowly lowered the casket lid—a moment of closure, both literally and figuratively.

The next day was the funeral, and frankly, I was ready for it all to be over and done with. I'd had enough at this point and was tired of feeling so heavy.

The weather that day was beautiful—a crisp, chilly November day, with not a single cloud in the sky. We arrived for the service at Saint Timothy's Episcopal Church—a church that held a special place in my parents' hearts because they had been part of a Monday night AA group there for years. I remember playing in the Sunday school classrooms of that church while my parents met down the hall.

Everyone was instructed to go to the outside chapel for the first part of the service. Cars began to pour into the parking lot of the small church, and before we knew it, over four hundred people were there. We honestly lost count.

We gathered in a large group at the outdoor chapel, and the reverend began by telling the story of Lynda, all those years ago at the VA, telling the intake officer about where he could stick his twenty-one guns. Her greatest desire was to be buried with full military honors but for the guns to remain silent.

My dad, Bridgid, and I stood in front of the large crowd while the dove guy handed us one single white dove. The next thing we knew, the dove man released twenty doves into the air. They flew above us and encircled us while people watched in awe. Despite the hundreds of people there, you could have heard a pin drop. Finally, the three of us released the final dove, which flew up and joined the other twenty. They flew in their perfect circle for a few minutes before flying off in a single-file line.

When I looked over, all of Mom's veteran friends in their uniforms stood in salute.

Tears streamed down people's faces, yet the funeral had barely even begun. We walked into the church for the service, and once the people finished pouring in—filling every row, seat, and corner of the sanctuary—we began the service.

My parents' friend Reverend William "Bill" Sproul did the invocation. Then my high school's a cappella choir, the Herndon High School Madrigals, sang two of my mom's favorite songs: "My Lord, What a Morning" and "Coventry Carol." In the weeks before she died, my mom would listen to me in my room as I practiced my parts for our upcoming choral performances. One day, I came down from my room to find my mom crying.

"What's wrong, Mom?"

"Your voice, singing my favorite carol . . . it's just so beautiful, honey."

"'Coventry Carol'? *That's* your favorite carol?"

"It always has been. It's so beautiful and haunting, and I love to hear your voice singing that song."

In case you're curious, the lyrics of "Coventry Carol" are as follows:

> *Lully, lullay, thou little tiny child,*
> *Bye bye, lully, lullay.*
> *Thou little tiny child,*
> *Bye bye, lully, lullay.*
> *O sisters too, how may we do*
> *For to preserve this day*
> *This poor youngling for whom we sing,*
> *"Bye bye, lully, lullay"?*
> *Herod the king, in his raging,*
> *Chargèd he hath this day*
> *His men of might in his own sight*
> *All young children to slay.*
> *That woe is me, poor child, for thee*

And ever mourn and may
For thy parting neither say nor sing,
"Bye bye, lully, lullay."

Mom never got to see me perform those songs live, so we sang them for her at her funeral instead.

The readings included Psalm 23 and Mom's poem "Making Friends." There was prayer, a blessing, and then the eulogies. My sister spoke, I spoke, a few of my friends spoke, and then her Vietnam friend Joan came up to speak. When Joan got to the front, she stood at the base of Mom's flag-draped casket and saluted. Every member of the military stood and did likewise. It was incredibly powerful.

Last, but certainly not least, it was time for my father to come up. He had been wrestling all week with what to say, and he'd especially struggled with anger and resentment toward those in Mom's life who had falsely accused her, abandoned her, and treated her so poorly over the years. Many of those people were in attendance that day, and my dad was less than pleased. He had a whole speech prepared about Lynda's strength—all she had gone through, the physical and emotional pain, and how she'd dealt with those who didn't understand. He wanted those who could not find the time to include her in their life to know what she'd experienced. In his eyes, she was the strongest woman he'd ever known.

But he changed course as he stood at the podium and looked out at the sanctuary, wall-to-wall with people. He thought, *No. These people are here to celebrate her. This isn't about the people who chose not to be a part of her life; it's about the people who did.*

He stared at the crowd for a while, gathering himself. And he began to speak. "Lynda and I knew this day would eventually come. We'd been somewhat prepared for a long time, having talked often about what this day might look like. So, I took some notes . . ." Then my father proceeded to grab an entire ream of computer paper from underneath the podium and slam it down in front of him.

The entire room erupted into laughter.

As you may recall, my mom was . . . let's say . . . detail-oriented.

Soon the noise died down, and Dad spoke again. "I'd planned to say something else," he said, "but as I stand here today, I wonder: How do we celebrate the life of a woman who was unlike any other? How do you honor someone for a job well done? Well, we give them a standing ovation."

My dad began to clap. And slowly, one by one, the entire church stood in applause. The roar of applause continued for what felt like ten minutes.

After that, my dad invited me up to the podium to sing my mom's favorite hymn, "Amazing Grace." I flashed back to those moments on Sunday mornings in the Black church down the road, my memory of Mom singing along to "Amazing Grace" with her eyes closed, the words knitting their way into our hearts. Somehow I stood there at the front of the room and I sang without an ounce of shake in my voice, and soon everyone else joined in.

I am still unsure how I got through that.

The service ended the way all AA meetings conclude: with the recitation of the Serenity Prayer, followed by the Lord's Prayer.§

Everyone got in their cars and headed to Chestnut Grove Cemetery. The funeral procession from the church to the cemetery was over three miles long. Do you know that scene at the end of the movie *Field of Dreams* where you can see the headlights of the cars streaming in for miles and miles? That's what it looked like as we stood at the graveside.

---

§ There *was* a "Keep comin' back. It works if you work it" ending this time.

The sun was setting as the flag-draped casket was placed on the bier. The final readings of the service were read. Mom's honor guard approached the casket, folded the flag, and presented it to Dad. Moments later, just off in the distance, underneath the branches of a large oak tree, Drew and Andrew began to play taps—the final piece of the military rights given to Mom. The last rays of the setting sun peered at us through the leaves.

Up until this point in the day, my emotions had been held under control. They had bubbled up like a kinked water hose, but in this moment, the feelings all came crashing through. The haunting melody of taps being played in the distance, the folded flag in my father's arms . . . The floodgates finally opened. I sobbed. My dad sobbed. Bridgid sobbed. Everyone sobbed.

And somehow, someway, we had to gather ourselves, leave the cemetery, and go home to eat country hams.[¶]

¶ To this very day, I cannot stand the smell or taste of a country ham.

12

THE WORLD IS NOT ENOUGH

NOVEMBER 21, 2002–AUGUST 22, 2006

Confidence is 10 percent hard work
and 90 percent delusion.

TINA FEY

Aside from having the country ham meat sweats, we spent the weeks and months after the funeral trying to get some sense of normalcy back. Dad and I went down to Raleigh, North Carolina, a week after the funeral to spend Thanksgiving with Bridgid. I ate more meat, binged *The Notebook* and *A Walk to Remember* by Nicholas Sparks, and spoke very little. Dad, Bridge, and I were all grieving in our own ways, and I think we just wanted to avoid talking about it. We could only lift the mood by telling a funny story about Mom or watching *Airplane!* for the thousandth time.

But after Dad and I got back to Jackson Street, everything was quiet. I went back to school. Dad worked, I think. I poured all my energy into choir and my new boyfriend. I kept busy and surrounded myself with friends and things to do, because if I slowed down or let myself be still, I would have to face my grief head-on.

A month after Mom died, Dad started traveling. He'd periodically go away for the weekend to play golf, visit someone, or do some professional training. Dad and I were always so close, but our grief became what I now realize was a wedge between us. We weren't hanging out as much as we used to, and we certainly weren't having any deep conversations. The distance between us continued to grow.

I also hated being in the house alone. I wouldn't go near Mom and Dad's room and physically couldn't step foot in their bathroom. Whenever I was in the house, I'd shut the doors to those rooms so I wouldn't have to look at them.

On one occasion, I was home alone, and the sliding door to the bathroom had been left open. When I walked by and caught a glimpse of the place where my mother had recently died, I collapsed and sobbed uncontrollably for hours. I couldn't move. I felt stuck on the floor, as if a giant anvil were on top of me.* Finally, when I gathered the strength to get up, this intense feeling of anger and rage welled up. I released a guttural, primal scream and slammed the sliding door shut so hard I knocked a picture frame off the wall.

For the rest of the time my dad owned Jackson Street, I avoided that room at all costs.

I was doing so well, thanks for noticing!

I also had to start thinking about college. That is, I had already been thinking about it, but college applications and the search process had all but halted in November, and deadlines were rapidly approaching.

My dad had pipe dreams of me playing golf in college and receiving

---

* In my mind, the anvil definitely had the "ACME" logo on it and Road Runner was somewhere nearby.

a scholarship offer from a school or two, but I'd reached a point in my golf career where I was too burned-out to compete in college. I really loved singing and acting and making people laugh, and I wanted to do some type of comedy. I knew *SNL* was the ultimate goal, but I hadn't a clue about how one even got there.

While my sister had gone to Virginia Tech, I didn't even apply because I was certain I wouldn't get in. I loved the school, but my SAT scores were . . . not great. I stumbled upon an "up-and-coming" university in Newport News, Virginia, called Christopher Newport University. It had been around for a couple of decades but was really gaining popularity, and I liked that it was a small public school. The campus was beautiful, and when I went to tour it, I discovered that CNU had a well-respected sketch comedy group too.

It was a sign! I submitted my application along with a killer essay, in the hopes that my amazing writing skills would offset my abysmal SAT score.

And they did.

A couple of weeks after submitting my application, I received a personal email from the dean of admissions at CNU telling me how much she'd loved my powerful essay. While I'd receive a formal letter in the mail soon, she wanted to let me know I had been accepted to the university. I was so excited, but at the same time I was devastated not to have Mom there to celebrate with me.

Once I got that college acceptance letter, I pretty much checked out for the rest of the school year. I wasn't going to fail my classes, but I definitely wasn't going to try hard. I was deeply sad. Aside from the incidents in preschool where I assaulted my teacher and sat on games, and the one time in fourth grade when I got sent to the principal's office for calling a boy in my class a sexist, I had always been a "good kid." I followed rules, I didn't drink or party, and I was trustworthy.

But all bets were off during that last semester of my senior year of high school. I started skipping school, going to parties, and making generally poor decisions. My dad had already started dating, which hurt me. I couldn't possibly understand why he wasn't still sad, but the truth was, he was lonely. I just couldn't see it. When I started writing this book, I sat down to have conversations with my dad and ask questions I should have asked twenty years ago. Now as an adult, I can understand some things much more than I did when I was seventeen and couldn't see through the fog of grief.

I was also becoming more and more angry, and I acted out by simply doing whatever felt good, promised fun, or seemed like a good idea at the time. If I didn't get caught, why did it matter? Until I did get caught . . . and, well, that may be another story for another book. (Or I'll tell you about it over tacos sometime.)

As a graduation present, my dad took some of the life insurance money he received from Mom's death and bought me my dream car: a manual transmission, sunshine-yellow, soft-top Jeep Wrangler. I couldn't believe it. I loved that Jeep so much and was so grateful for it, but looking back, I regret not expressing to my dad how much that Jeep meant to me.

Graduation came and went, I worked all summer at the golf course and a local spa, and my boyfriend, James, and I spent as much of our free time together as we could. Seeing as how he was a year younger than me, he'd be staying in Herndon come August to start his senior year, and I would be headed off to CNU. We decided to try the long-distance thing, hoping we could make it work.

In August, I said goodbye to James. Then Dad and I packed up my things and drove to Newport News to move me into my dorm. The anticipation of going off to college was fraught with mixed emotions. I was really afraid of leaving my dad, and even though we'd grown more distant since Mom's death, I knew that my moving out would be really hard on him (and me, for that matter). I hated to think about him being all alone back in Herndon. At the same time, I couldn't wait to start college.

College was a chance to reinvent myself. The people I would soon meet wouldn't know the old me. They wouldn't know who I was. I focused on a fresh start, a new life. This was Molly 2.0.

This was my chance to be successful, to be popular, to be cool, to be accepted. It's not that I didn't have friends in high school; I did, and they were awesome! I was well liked in high school, but I was never popular—something I so badly wanted. I got pretty good grades, but I was never smart. I wasn't in honors classes or AP classes. I wasn't in any honor societies or in the gifted and talented program. I was average. The only thing I was voted in high school was "Class Clown" in the senior superlatives—so college was my chance to prove I was funny *and* a leader.

I was going to take CNU by storm.

Many kids, especially those who are grieving or compensating for something, go off the rails in college with parties or boys or general raucous behavior.

Not yours truly. The day after I settled into my dorm, I registered to run for freshman class president (an election I won by a landslide). I went to the informational meeting for the sketch comedy group CNU TONiGHT (which I promptly joined and started submitting sketches for). I took myself on a tour of campus to find my classes and introduce myself to my professors (then got nearly all As my first semester). I went through Greek rush and joined a sorority (go Phi Mu!).

I was killing it.

I was doing exactly what I knew I could do: proving to myself and everyone that I *was* smart, cool, funny, successful, and popular.

I started the year with musical theater as my major, thinking that if I honed my singing and acting skills, they would help me with my comedy career. But when I sat down with my academic advisor in the theater department, he asked me what I was involved in.

"Well, I've rushed a sorority, I'm class president, and I've become a writer and performer in the campus sketch comedy group CNU TONiGHT!" I said excitedly.

"CNU TONiGHT?" he asked with a tinge of judgment, as he peered over his glasses that rested on the bridge of his nose.

"Yes, I love it! My dream is to be on *SNL*, so I thought that between musical theater and CNU TONiGHT I would be well prepared for New York after college," I responded confidently.

"Oh, no, no, no. This will not work," he bellowed. "CNU TONiGHT is a mockery of the theater.† Any *real* thespian would know that sketch comedy is *not* acting. It's buffoonery at best. You will have to decide between the two. Do you want to do real theater, or go off with those clowns?"

I sat stunned. I took a breath and replied, "Well, looks like it's all the buffoonery for me."

I got up and walked out. Then I went to the academic affairs office and changed my major to English with a concentration in creative writing.

I'll show him a real thespian! I thought.

I worked really hard at working hard. But on the inside, I was miserable.

When the first anniversary of Mom's death arrived, I didn't even want to talk about it. Dad was still dating, and it was getting pretty

---

† If you pronounced the word *theater* as "THEE-YUH-TUH" in your head as you read that, you would be correct. He was not British, but that's how he said *theater*. That should have really been my clue to leave.

serious. The next thing I knew, he told me he and his girlfriend were building a house in Florida.

Florida.

He was moving to Florida.

With a woman who wasn't my mom.

He was building a house.

In Florida.

He told me we'd be spending Christmas at the new house in Florida. Christmas. In Florida. My first Christmas not in Herndon, in the house I grew up in, in the house my parents married in, in the house my mom died in.

Florida was not close to Virginia. Florida was . . . *Florida.* I put on a brave face and told him I was happy for him, but I was crushed.

———

The end of my freshman year of college came, and though I was sad to be leaving for the summer, I was really excited to go home and see James. He'd come to visit me a couple of times, but we hadn't seen each other much since I went to college. We mostly communicated through AOL Instant Messenger (my screen name was CNUMoLLy‡) and through phone calls because texting cost approximately $750 per message back then.

He graduated shortly after I got home, then he proceeded to break up with me because he wanted to be single and *keep his options open* when he went away to college.

What? I stayed with you when I went away to school! You couldn't do me the same decency? I was hurt, and I was also mad.

---

‡ I changed my screen name *all the time.* Past screen names included OLdNaVyAnGeL, MoLLyoLLy2, and AnGeLL823.

I worked all summer at the golf course with my dad, and at night I waitressed at a local TGI Fridays (complete with a few pieces of flair!) to make as much money as possible before going back to school in August.

For my sophomore and junior years of college, I kept on a similar path of working hard in the classroom, making myself known around campus in positions of leadership, loving my friends in Phi Mu, and falling in love with a boy. I had "made it." I had reinvented myself. I was finally everything I hadn't been in middle and high school.

The persona I had worked so hard to build and maintain was everything to me.

Until it wasn't.

13

GO BIG OR GO ROME!

AUGUST 24, 2006–MAY 13, 2007

The wise store up choice food and olive
oil, but fools gulp theirs down.

PROVERBS 21:20

Remember that thing I told you about at the very start of this book? I left you on a bit of a cliffhanger, and since we are good friends by this point of our journey . . . it's probably time I pick back up where we left off.

I mean, besides being late to class, what *did* I do with all that money?

No one sets a goal like: "I think I'd like to squander a small fortune this year." Coming into a whirlwind of financial abundance is an odd thing. I don't think anyone can ever prepare for such an event, but when it's unexpected and you're ill-equipped, it's truly a recipe for disaster.

At twenty-one years old, I hadn't the slightest clue how to go about managing my finances. For much of my life, I lived in a perpetual "deal with what's in front of me" state of mind. People change. Plans change. Life circumstances change. So why would I need to bother with preparing for the future? I mean, sure, I was in college to get a degree and hopefully set myself up for long-term career success—but really, college was a placeholder until I could find stardom on *Saturday Night Live.* My circumstances meant that finances just weren't . . . top of mind for me.

I feel like this is obvious to say at this point, but I really did have the most incredible parents growing up. They were in love, they loved me, they were caring and selfless, they were hilarious and honest. They were amazing, but they were not perfect. All that being said, I cannot, to my best attempt, recall any real conversations about managing money.

Here's what I knew about money growing up:

- Money was tight.
- Thrift shopping was our MO (long before shopping second-hand was considered trendy).
- I knew about "snack bucks." Snack bucks were one-dollar bills my dad would drop me from time to time when I was getting out of the car at school. Snack bucks were only to be used for snacks from the vending machine outside the school gym. If the vending machine didn't snack on my snack bucks and I actually got what I wanted, my snacks of choice were a honey bun or a bag of Cheez-It crackers. If I was feeling frisky, and if the inventory cooperated, I might get some brown sugar Pop-Tarts.
- I received an allowance of twenty dollars, but it was not on a schedule of any sort.

- My parents made me work for under-the-table money before I was of age.
- As soon as I was of age, my parents made me get a "real" job.
- I knew how to write a check.
- I knew I could get a free T-shirt for signing up for a Capital One credit card.
- Annnnd . . . that's about it. I didn't know how to budget. I didn't know how to invest. I didn't know how to save. But I sure knew how to spend!

So when I suddenly received a check for nearly a quarter of a million dollars, I was relatively uncertain about what the heck I should do with it. I mean that both in a literal and a figurative sense.

A few factors came into play:

I felt really uncomfortable walking around campus with this *massive* check in my possession, so I knew I needed to unload that thing . . . STAT.

I also was hyperaware that any public knowledge of my sudden windfall should be averted if possible, so I was especially careful about whom I told. It wasn't as simple as going up to my friends and saying, "You'll *never* guess what I got today."

I felt paralyzed with fear, elation, and what-in-the-world-is-happening.

I knew I needed help, so I called my dad.

"Uhhh . . . hi, Dad!"

"Hi, honey. Happy birthday!"

"So, uhhh, how's Florida?" I deferred.

"It's good. You okay? You sound funny."

"Yeah, I'm, uhhh . . . I'm good. So, question for you . . . if one were to receive a check for a quarter of a million dollars, what would one do with it?" I blurted out.

"Molly, you got what? Is that the check from Rodney and Helen's trust? I didn't think that was happening!" He seemed shocked.

"Yeah. Yeah it has . . . it is, rather."

"Wow. Well, I'm so happy for you, sweetheart. That's great. Well . . . *wow*. Okay. Couple things: Your tuition is due, so you should pay that now. And you probably should take that check down to the bank and talk to a teller there. Okay?"

"Yeah, yeah okay. That's it?" I replied.

"Yes, go do that. Talk to you soon, sweetheart! Love you!"

"Ohhhhkay, Dad. Love you too."

So that afternoon, I did the only thing I knew to do: I marched to the Bank of America down the road. I walked through the glass and metal doors that screamed for a shot of WD-40, and the aroma of lemongrass and sage assaulted me. You know, the "bank smell." (Is it just me, or do all banks smell the same?) I walked up to the counter and said, "Hi. I need some help depositing this check."

The teller looked at me, looked down at the check, and with wide eyes and a pandering voice and thick southern drawl, said, "I think you should take this to our banking specialist over there."

Moseys over to the banking specialist

The banking specialist, we'll call him "Frank," sat at his desk typing away, completely ignoring me as I stood right in front of him. He looked up through his thin-framed, split-front readers and seemed genuinely annoyed at my presence.

"Hi, excuse me. I need some help depositing this check."

"Please go see the teller, ma'am."

"The teller sent me to you, sir," I responded with a tinge of sarcasm.

He sighed as he took the check from my hands. Then he looked down at the check, looked up at me, looked down at the check, looked up at me . . . down, up, down, up.

"Ma'am, is this check legitimate?" Frank questioned.

"Um, yes? I have a pile of documents from a law firm in DC that goes along with it . . . if you need to see it," I replied.

What I really wanted to say was "Do you find yourself faced with a lot of twenty-one-year-old girls trying to commit check fraud?"

"Okay, well, how are you going to need to access this money? Do you need it liquid?" Frank asked.

I stared at him.

"Liquid? I don't need to drink my money, Mr. Frank. I mean, sir."

"No, ma'am. Liquid, as in, how much of it do you need to access right now or in the near future?" he quipped.

"Well, I need money for my tuition payments for the rest of this year, I'd like to give some of this money to my dad and sister, and I'd like to start a scholarship in my mom's name at my university. But I haven't the foggiest clue as to what to do with the rest. Should I save some? Can someone put the rest in a savings account? Should I look into stocks or something? What's a 401(k)? I think I heard something about an NRA once . . . or maybe an IRA? Do I need that?"

I sputtered off questions like the engine on my 1993 Ford Escort.

Frank looked at me like I was a complete idiot and responded with "Yes, you should save some money." He paused for a few moments to think. "Okay, here's what we're going to do, Ms. Buckley. We're going to take fifteen thousand of this and set it aside for your tuition, room, and board for the remainder of the year and place it in your checking account. You might want to go ahead and write one check to cover it all and drop it off at the finance office. I will set aside seventy thousand for your dad and sister. We'll put around eighty thousand in different increments into some CDs,* and the rest we'll keep liquid in a savings account."

---

* If you don't know about CDs, they are "certificates of deposit." Basically, they're near-worthless long-term savings accounts.

"But what about the scholarship I want to start?" I said.

"Well, Ms. Buckley, starting scholarships is not part of my job description, so you'll need to figure that out yourself. When you drop off that tuition check at the finance office, why don't you ask to speak with someone who deals in scholarships? That's why we'll put the remainder of the funds in your savings account," he said.

"Um, okay," I relented.

"I'll be right back," Frank said.

He got up from his desk and walked to the back. He meandered around in no hurry at all, stopping to talk to his colleagues. He'd mumble something to them, and they'd immediately turn to look at me. While I don't want to speculate that it was *all* about me, it certainly didn't feel awesome to have everyone in the building staring and gawking.

After what felt like forty-five minutes, Frank returned with a stack of papers in his left hand and a refilled, steaming coffee in his right. He slammed the paperwork down, slid it in my direction, and told me to sign by the little colored tabs.

I signed the paperwork, handed over the endorsed check, bid my adieu to Frank, and walked out of the building.

And that, ladies and gentlemen, is the first and the last of the financial advice I received that day about managing a quarter of a million dollars. Even now, I have absolutely no idea what in the world Frank the "banking specialist" was thinking.

Look, I need to make this clear: I 100 percent own every mistake I made. I take full ownership of the mess I created for myself. I understand that my choices were mine, and I was an adult woman who had to learn somehow. But it still boggles my ever-loving mind that this man, a "banking specialist" in his midfifties, couldn't (or wouldn't) look at precious, doe-eyed, twenty-one-year-old me and say,

"You should probably speak with a financial advisor about your long-term financial future."

The irony is not lost on me that I'm now married to a financial advisor.

Or! *Or! OR!* How about taking a moment to give me real, *actual* financial advice? How? HOW?! Why?! *Why, oh, whyyyy* did this man not ask me real, hard-hitting questions about what I wanted to do with the money? Or maybe, just maybe, he could have suggested I think about the future for a millisecond. Perhaps he could have walked me out the squeaky bank doors, slapped me on the rear, and said, "Don't be an idiot by squandering all this money in the next two years!"

Nope. That would have been too easy. And come to think of it, inappropriate.

There I was, a fresh twenty-one-year-old with no financial experience, receiving absolutely zero guidance from an ignoramus of a banking specialist, carrying a whole lot of life baggage, searching for purpose and meaning and identity, walking out of a Bank of America with a tidy sum of cash.

I went back to my apartment that afternoon, collapsed on my bed, and stared up at the popcorn ceiling, thinking, *What the heck do I do now?*

That night I went for a walk on campus in a feeble attempt to clear my head. None of this felt real, none of it made sense, and I felt really odd. I had a pit in my stomach that made me feel sick. I missed my mom so much. I couldn't help but think, *This is her money. I don't deserve this. She should be here.*

I missed her on my birthday. I missed hearing her laugh. I missed her advice. I just really missed her. I ran the gamut of emotions that night, from elated to depressed to angry to confused to terrified to melancholic.

I'd already called my dad, and I didn't have anyone else on earth to actually talk to about this. Trying to process the events of the past twelve hours felt incredibly overwhelming, and I wound up sobbing on a bench near the school gym. I was searching for hope in things that could not give me hope. I was so lost.

I wasn't conscious of it at the time, but getting that money was the genesis of a pattern of isolating myself from others. I couldn't possibly let anyone know the real me, the true me, the deepest, darkest parts of me. I had to face this on my own. I had gotten myself this far, so I could carry myself the rest of the way!

The only emotional coping tool I possessed was the tried-and-true "disregard and distract" method: *If I pretend everything's fine, then everything will be fine!* The problem was, that method wasn't foolproof. It was just proof that I was a fool.

The next day, I woke up and did what any other completely un-restricted, emotionally unstable human with no self-control would do: I swaggered my butt down to the local Jeep dealership and, *like an idiot*, traded in my dream car, my yellow 2001 Jeep Wrangler, for a brand-new, black, limited edition 2007 Jeep Commander with tan leather interior.

Writes a check for $40,000 like it ain't no thang

Forty. Grand. Out the window in a flash. (I still regret this deci-sion to this day.)

But *holy smokes*, that Jeep was *noice*. I thought I was hot stuff. The hottest of stuff.

Twenty-four hours earlier, I had been so concerned about keeping this news quiet. And now . . . how on earth would I explain away my brand-new $40,000 Jeep? My SGA president stipend wasn't cov-ering such a purchase. Employ the disregard and distract method! When asked, I just confidently replied, "Oh this? I saved up! It was a birthday present for me! Let's go get some Mexican food!" And somehow, people just . . . believed it? Truly, I have no idea.

The dopamine hit I got from heedlessly buying that Jeep ignited something in me. I'd spent the better part of twenty-one years shopping at Kmart or working multiple jobs. I'd dreamt of being able to walk into a place and just buy the thing I wanted without giving it a second thought. So, all of a sudden, knowing I *could* do that became instantly addicting.

Some ways people knowingly or unknowingly cope with depression, anxiety, or stress include avoidance, excessive drinking, drug use, or risky behavior. While avoidance was certainly one of my long-loved coping mechanisms, the riskier behaviors weren't issues for me. But suddenly, I'd found something that made me feel better momentarily: *spending money*. It also wasn't harming anyone! It was safe! It was effective! It provided dopamine hit after dopamine hit.

I now had a coping mechanism for my deep-seated issues!

When I was sad, I spent money. When I got mad, I spent money. When I was happy, I spent money. When I was celebrating, I spent money. When I was scared, I spent money. When I missed my mom, I spent money. When my boyfriend and I argued, I spent money. My response to just about any and every feeling was to spend money.

For Christmas break that year, I opted to register for multiple improv comedy classes at the Upright Citizens Brigade Theatre in New York City. I flew myself up there and stayed with my cousin Meredith who lived in Manhattan, and during my free time I went out to eat, explored the city, went shopping, and spent more money.

As I walked up and down Fifth Avenue, I'd walk into designer stores and feel this sense of power. It was an illusion of control I'd never experienced before. I walked into the Fendi store and saw the most beautiful handbag I'd ever laid my eyes on, like Aladdin spotting the lamp in the Cave of Wonders for the first time. The light shone directly on it, and I could have sworn I heard a choir of angels singing faintly in the distance. The purse was a rosy-pink leather saddle bag with a brown-and-tan FENDI cross-stitch and a gold buckle. The price tag: $2,735. I glided over, put the bag in my hands, zoomed to the counter, and bought it.

For spring break, I decided to go big or go Rome—as in Rome, Italy, not Rome, Georgia. Without hesitating, I booked a trip for my boyfriend, Derek, and me to fly to Rome. When we got to the airport, I walked up to the ticket counter and decided on a whim to upgrade us to first class. Because why not?

We happened to miss our connecting flight in Philadelphia, so we arrived in Rome a day late with our luggage missing. The airline had no clue where our bags were. All we had were our backpacks and the pajamas on our backs. Yes, we wore pajamas on the airplane. I'm not talking sweatpants or stylish loungewear. I'm telling you, my boyfriend wore plaid flannel pj pants and a spray-painted shirt, and I wore pajama pants with pink monkeys on them, a sorority Greek-letter T-shirt, and a Victoria's Secret PINK hoodie.

With our luggage nowhere to be found, I got us a taxi to the shopping district of Rome because we needed *something* to wear. There was no Roman Walmart to waltz into. Nope. We had Calvin Klein, Prada, or Gucci. With my options limited, I bought us jeans and shirts from Calvin Klein to hold us off until our luggage arrived.

———

I spent money, and I spent more money.

It never occurred to me for even a fleeting second that I should keep track of the money leaving my account. It never occurred to me to budget. It never occurred to me to read my bank statements. It never occurred to me that my choices were destructive.

Not until the end of my senior year did I realize something could be amiss.

When I'd approached the university finance office at the beginning of the year about creating the scholarship fund, they said we could iron out the details at some point during the year to finalize the fund before graduation. When it came time actually to write that check for the scholarship, I realized I didn't have access to the cash. I'd given my dad and sister some money, I'd put a lot of the money in CDs I didn't want to touch, and I'd spent the rest of what I had on New York and Rome and heaven-knows-what. The amount of money in my checking and savings accounts was low. So I looked at the only "liquid" thing I owned: my brand-new $40,000 Jeep Commander. I got that sinking feeling in my chest, but I swallowed my pride, sold the Jeep for something cheaper, and wrote the check for the scholarship.

When my friends asked, "Why'd you sell your new Jeep, Molly? Didn't you just get that in August?" I'd explain it away and say, "Yeah, it was too much car for me! I don't need seven seats!" I took the remaining amount of money and bought a Volkswagen Rabbit.

You'd think that a mere nine months with that car and having to sell it would have woken me up to my spending habits. *Oh, you-of-too-much-faith-in-me.*

It sure did not. I went right back to spending and spending.

Disregard and distract!

14

GRADUATION SONG

MAY 13, 2007

It turns out, being an adult is mostly
just googling how to do stuff.

UNKNOWN

When you're in the thick of school, you aren't fully aware of how much your life will change when you graduate. Now I know why there are a bunch of songs about school graduations . . . and only one (at least that I know of) about hot cross buns.

College is amazing. I loved college. Living surrounded by friends, having no real-world responsibilities beyond paying a cell phone bill or working at a local crab restaurant, taking classes about things you're actually interested in, staying up late, sleeping 'til noon, eating cheese fries for breakfast, pulling all-nighters fueled by a steady stream of Diet Coke and Fun Dip, being game for Mexican food every night of the week—and it's all socially acceptable!

Then, suddenly, you leave college and are thrust into a world where—generally speaking—you have to find a place to live, pay bills, start a career, make good choices, pay taxes, get your oil changed, find a doctor who's not your pediatrician, worry about cholesterol, take vitamins that aren't shaped like Wilma and Fred Flintstone, make sure you have ibuprofen in your purse *and* at home, stop drinking beverages out of a bathtub in a fraternity house . . . *It's a big change!*

Some have a slow transition from college to adulthood. Mine was not.

I graduated from Christopher Newport University on Sunday, May 13, 2007, packed up my things, and moved to Richmond, Virginia, the next day to start a fellowship program working for then governor of Virginia Tim Kaine. I'd applied to be in the Governor's Fellows Program at the suggestion of one of my political science teachers. It was a really competitive program that thousands of kids from across the state applied to, and fewer than thirty were accepted. I thought there was no way I'd get it, but somehow, I did.

The program didn't pay, but I received a small stipend to cover the basic cost of living while participating. But, since I was still in a downward spiraling pattern of spending, I paid no attention to my lack of income and rented myself a fancy one-bedroom apartment in downtown Richmond. I also needed new clothes because I was working for the governor, after all . . . so I went down to Saks Fifth Avenue and dropped a thousand dollars on power suits.

I was assigned to the governor's policy office, where I'd spend the next eight weeks. There I would work right alongside the governor's staff and cabinet members, observing the inner workings of the executive branch of Virginia government. My desk was in a small, windowless room right around the corner from Governor Kaine's office, and I'd sometimes get to bring him a Diet Dr Pepper or walk by his office and catch him playing his harmonica or jamming out to some Dave Matthews Band.

My work included researching for policy initiatives, attending cabinet or committee meetings, and dealing with constituent correspondence. I actually really enjoyed the policy research and constituent correspondence pieces. I had access to an entire database where literally every email, physical letter, or voicemail from Virginia constituents was cataloged. This was less than two months after the horrific shootings at Virginia Tech, and much of the communication was about that. I was fascinated by the logistics of it all.

In the correspondence office, where I filed things and located form letters for responses, I also discovered the *autopen*. The autopen machine was programmed with the governor's signature, so I could put any writing utensil in the machine and have it sign his signature perfectly, every time. I would take sticky notes and random documents, write notes on them to myself, and then autopen Tim Kaine's signature.[*]

You are amazing! —Tim Kaine
You are the funniest person I've ever met! —Tim Kaine
You don't have to pay state taxes ever again! —Tim Kaine

The fellowship would last only two months, though we all hoped we would get hired at the end of it. The reality was, those of us who'd graduated that year were entering one of the most challenging job markets in decades. The economy was on the downswing, budget cuts were happening left and right, and the competition was fierce. Our more realistic hope was that the fellowship would be the résumé booster we needed to get hired somewhere else.

I loved working for Governor Kaine, but I felt so out of place. Everyone I worked with was buttoned-up, serious about pursuing a

---

[*] For legal purposes: I never used the autopen to my own personal advantage. I did, however, use the autopen for my own personal amusement.

career in politics or the public sector, and I wanted to be . . . a sketch comedian. I mean, I loved politics. I had been a political science minor and heavily involved in student government in college, so I was knowledgeable and capable enough—but I didn't know where I belonged. I was a fish out of water. I did my best and worked hard, hoping I'd figure out what the heck I was doing somewhere along the way.

While I wore a suit by day, by night I was getting involved in the local Richmond improv comedy scene and flexing my comedy writing muscles by publishing satire pieces on my new blog. I loved writing. During my junior year of college, I'd started writing on a LiveJournal website—which was basically a blog before blogs really existed. I mostly wrote down Dave Matthews or Dashboard Confessional lyrics, but I toyed around with writing satire or parody pieces too.

During my senior year, one of my creative writing classes for my major encouraged us to write daily on a blog. Whether it was a poem, a journal entry, a satire, whatever . . . my professor didn't care. She said, "Just open up a new page and write. Every single day. The only way you're going to get better as a writer is to write."

So I did. I loved it. That blog became the place where I could safely toss around ideas or get my creative juices flowing. It became a much-needed creative outlet for me. No one knew what a blog was,[†] but I loved writing mine. When I'd come home from improv rehearsal or a show, I'd sit at my laptop, take an idea or scene I'd done that night, and try to flesh it out into a sketch or a story.

I thought if I built some massive portfolio of writing samples and sketches, the work would somehow pay off and make it easier to get hired doing comedy. After work at the governor's office, if we didn't have some event or social that night, I would spend hours writing and

---

† I remember my roommate Jane Berry asking me "What in the world is a WEBLOG? Do people actually read those things?"

searching for jobs in New York. I signed up for improv and comedy writing classes in the city for later that summer. I invited my boyfriend, Derek, and my best guy friend, Bryan, to go with me, and they were up for it. Derek had started doing comedy with me later in college, and though he really enjoyed it, he'd never tried improv before. Bryan and I met my freshman year in our campus sketch comedy group, CNU TONiGHT. By our senior year, he and I were like brother and sister and did a lot of comedy writing together. We used to think of ourselves as the on-campus version of Tina Fey and Jimmy Fallon.

I was trying to exhaust all options because I had no idea what I was going to do once my fellowship ended.

About a month into the fellowship, my boss said he needed to speak with me in his office. As an Enneagram two, any instance in which someone says "we need to talk" is my actual worst nightmare.

I went into his office and sat down. "You asked to see me, Mr. Davis?"

"Yes, Molly. I want to thank you for your effort here in Governor Kaine's office. You're working very hard, and the work you're producing is top-notch. However, I need to tell you that your laughter is disturbing the office. This is the office of the governor of Virginia. You laugh very loudly, and it's disruptive to others around you. You do not take yourself seriously enough, and this is a serious place to work, so I would advise you to tighten up and remember what your purpose is here. It is not to joke around."

I thought he was pulling my leg at first, that this was one of those "You're too fun!" bits. I wish this story was a joke. I smiled at him but then realized he was very much *not* smiling back at me. My face turned red and my chest got hot.

I had no idea what to say. I was crushed. My whole life, I'd felt like I was "too much." I'd gotten in trouble countless times in school for laughing too much or too loudly. It was genetics! *Had no one even met my family of Irish Catholics?* They were all loud laughers. I was never being "bad" or intentionally trying to get myself in trouble; I was just being myself. I'd spent so much effort trying to tone myself down for everyone around me. And there I was, once again, being told I was too much.

It took every last ounce of willpower I had to not burst into tears at that moment. I shook my head in understanding and said, "Yes, sir, Mr. Davis. I'll do my best not to disrupt the office."

I walked out of his office and *then* burst into tears. I hustled down the hallway, trying to make my way to the bathroom, when I *literally* bumped into Governor Kaine.

"Oh, gosh, Governor Kaine, I'm so sorry! I didn't see you!" I couldn't look up at him as I wiped tears from my eyes.

He was holding a stack of papers. "It's okay!" he said. "It's Molly, right? You're in our fellows program. How are you enjoying it?"

"Yes, sir. Yes, I am. I'm enjoying it very much." I looked up and knew he could tell I wasn't okay.

"Molly, are you okay? What happened?" he asked earnestly.

"Well, honestly, I was told today—and I wish I was joking here—that my laughter is too loud for the office. Apparently I need to take my job here more seriously. I . . . I am so sorry. I apologize if I've ever been disruptive. It wasn't my intention . . ." I stammered.

"Molly, please don't apologize. I don't know what happened, but I can assure you, your joy here is contagious—and some of the people in this office could stand to lighten up a little. Don't ever let anyone tell you you're too much and that your laughter isn't God-given. He's given you that gift . . . it's your job to steward it well," he said. "Have a great day, Molly."

And he walked away. I stood in disbelief. No one had ever told me that something like my laugh, my sense of humor, was "God-given." It had always felt like a liability.

While I'd initially felt so defeated, I now felt encouraged that maybe, just maybe, I was moving in the right direction.

———

I was rejected for every job I applied for in New York. I knew I couldn't move without a job because, even though I was incredibly reckless with money, the cost of rent in New York was so astronomical I knew I'd last only a month or two before winding up on the streets.

The clock was ticking on my fellowship, and I had to start thinking about what to do next. Working in the governor's policy office, I'd been attending committee meetings with the secretary of education. In one of those meetings, I'd happened to sit next to the superintendent of Henrico County Public Schools, and we'd had a few great conversations over the course of a couple of weeks.

One day at the end of a meeting, he stood up, walked over to me, and asked, "What are you planning to do after your fellowship is over, Molly?"

"I have no idea. I'm going to New York City at the beginning of August to take some comedy classes and look for a job, but other than that, I'm not sure," I replied honestly.

"Have you ever considered teaching?" he asked point-blank.

"Teaching? But I didn't go to college to be a teacher. Plus, I'm trying to get into comedy. That doesn't exactly seem like a natural progression," I responded.

"Well," he said, "we need teachers right now, and I think you'd be a phenomenal teacher. We have a lateral entry program where you can become certified to teach while you are teaching. You can teach in the area your degree is in." He paused. "Look, I had to ask because I think you'd be really great. Give it some thought. I know you're going to New York, but if you don't find a job, please call me when you get back."

He handed me his card and walked out of the meeting.

Before that day, I'd never remotely considered teaching as a career choice. It wasn't even on my radar. But something about what he said stuck with me, and I didn't rule it out as an option.

My fellowship ended, I didn't get a job in the governor's office, and I hopped on a bus to New York with Derek and Bryan. We were headed up to take a ten-day intensive sketch and improv comedy class through the New York chapter of the Second City Training Center.

We did it all on a shoestring budget. We took the Chinatown bus up and back from DC (forty bucks round trip!) and stayed in an eight-dollars-per-night hostel on the Upper East Side of Manhattan in a shared room with eight bunk beds. Needless to say, the conditions of the hostel lent themselves to some unique experiences. No, we were not lured into some room to be tortured and murdered. Since Bryan, Derek, and I were in the eight-person bunk room staying for an extended period, the remaining five beds were a revolving door of interesting characters.

For example, we spent one night with five French women who were presumably in town auditioning for a modeling gig. We awoke in the morning to them talking with each other, entirely nude. I looked over to find Bryan and Derek in their bunks trying to pretend they were asleep, but they absolutely were not. I looked at Derek and was like, "*HELLO! OVER HERE, BUDDY!*"

There was the punk band who smelled like months-old BO and cheese, the international students who needed a place to stay before starting at Columbia University, the guy in town auditioning for some kind of opera who sang loudly almost the entire time he was there ... We also had some genuinely cool people who stayed in the room, but those were few and far between.

In the city, I'd reached out to multiple places searching for jobs, but every door I opened was slammed in my face. Something in me knew it wasn't the right time and I was supposed to wait to move.

Derek and I were also nearing the end of our relationship rope—arguing and fighting a lot on the trip.

The more I thought about it, the more I knew I should stay in Richmond at least another year or two. I got home from New York, broke up with Derek, called the superintendent, set up a job interview, and was hired days later for a job at a local high school teaching tenth-grade English and photojournalism. They also had an opening for a varsity golf coach. Barely four weeks after ending my fellowship and two weeks after returning home from New York, I was turning twenty-two years old and starting my first day as a high school teacher. I stood in my new classroom, terrified and hopeful. I had zero clue what I was doing, but this small "win" made me feel, momentarily, like I was doing the right thing. Also, the chance to shop for school supplies helped. I love school supplies.

For the next nine months, I refused to acknowledge the damage I was doing to myself. I had a real job! I was a teacher! I was a grown-up now! Any chance I got, I'd spend money to self-medicate. Shopping, taking more trips to New York, chaperoning a field trip to Costa Rica, renting a way-too-expensive apartment, going out to bars with friends on the weekends, shopping more ... What did it matter if I was out of control in my spending? What did it matter if I was meeting random guys at bars on the weekends? What did it matter if I was staying out way too late after comedy shows? Nothing I did was "that bad." It could be "worse." I still had my life "together."

I was spiraling out of control, chasing after worldly idols like fame, fortune, men, and status. I avoided looking in the mirror and really doing any kind of self-examination about who I was, what I was doing, or where I was headed. The lower I felt about myself, the more I'd compensate by doing the quick thing that made me "feel good."

Ignorance was bliss.

That is, until it wasn't.

15

BROKE(N)

JUNE 14, 2008

The wicked borrow and do not repay,
but the righteous give generously.

PSALM 37:21

My palms were sweaty. My knees were weak. My arms were heavy. There was no vomit on my sweater already, and I had not had anyone's mom's spaghetti. (Stop me if you've heard this one.) The words of the great Marshall Bruce Mathers III could not have rung more true for me that day.

I sat down at my desk and faced the stack of bills I'd been avoiding for weeks. As I opened each one, that hot, sinking feeling radiated throughout my chest and into my stomach. You know exactly the feeling I'm talking about; it's the feeling you get when your boss says, "We need to talk." Or the feeling you got when your parents caught you doing something and said they weren't mad, just disappointed. Or the feeling you get when you realize your toddler somehow just uploaded a picture they took of you half naked to your Instagram story. (Just me?)

Now, I'm not a math person,* seeing as how I got my degree in English with a concentration in creative writing—but as I opened every bill and statement, I saw the bold type on each one:

PAST DUE.

LIMIT REACHED.

WILL BE SENT TO COLLECTIONS SOON.

OVERDRAFTED.

YOU ARE A TERRIBLE MONEY MANAGER AND

A HORRIBLE, HORRIBLE HUMAN BEING. HOW

COULD YOU NOT SEE THIS COMING?!

Maybe that last one wasn't there, but you get my point. The numbers and letters seemed to physically come off the page like they do in cartoons, enlarging in tandem with my bulging eyeballs as they registered how much debt I was in.

I looked at my empty savings account (which was supposed to have enough money to cover any checking overdrafts), and my checking account read: "-$128." Great. I *owed* the bank $128. About half of that was just from overdraft fees.

Fantastic.

Until then, I truly had no clue how bad my debt actually was. I knew it was thousands-of-dollars bad, but I had no idea *how many* thousands. I only tended to look at my bank account whenever my credit card got declined, which was happening more than usual. I'd

---

* By "not a math person," I mean that I am hilariously terrible at math. My friends and family like to poke fun at me for just how bad I am. My husband likes to regularly quiz me on my multiplication tables. At the time of this writing, I am thirty-eight and still don't know them all.

avoided it long enough and simply couldn't avoid it any longer. My poor choices finally had caught up with me.

Everything started to spin. I shut the door to my room so my roommate wouldn't know what was going on. I dropped to the floor, and without realizing it, curled up in the fetal position. As I rocked back and forth, my vision clouded.

I shook.

I twitched.

I cried.

I panted.

I rocked.

I had a full-blown panic attack.

I'd had only one other panic attack in my life, but that's how I knew I was having another one.

In that moment, I felt more alone, more ashamed, and more guilty than ever before. Because the reality was, I had put myself in this position. This rock bottom was the fallout from my irresponsibility, my dumb decisions, my own actions. I was a statistic . . . I had squandered away hundreds of thousands of dollars and buried myself so deeply in a hole that I thought I'd never claw my way out. For the better part of two years, I'd made decision after decision completely disconnected from reality, with zero regard for the consequences. Yet none of the decisions, on the surface, seemed like they were all that bad at the time. Talk about death by a thousand cuts.

I had no idea where to turn and no clue how to get myself out of the financial, personal, and relational mess I'd created. Shame kept me from calling my dad or my sister, because then they'd know what I'd done. Embarrassment kept me from asking any friends for help. I was on a desert island of my own making.

I felt like I'd let everyone down, and even worse, I just knew my

mom was up in heaven looking down on me . . . not mad, but disap-
pointed† with what should have been *her* money. How could I have
been so selfish? How could I have been so irresponsible? How could I
have been so stupid? I felt like I'd let my mom down, and she would've
been so ashamed of me.

There was only one logical next step. I contemplated suicide.

In a moment of desperation and as a last-ditch effort, I picked up
the phone and called my bank. I figured the first step would be to
cry, scream, beg, plead, or negotiate for the overdraft charges on my
account to be lifted—for the fourth time in two months. I had no idea
if it would work, but I could only try.

By the time I got to the customer service rep on the other end of
the line, she picked up and so sweetly said, "Thank you for calling
BB&T. My name is Janet. How may I assist you today?"

To which I replied: "*WAHHHHHHHHHHHHHHHHH.*" Dear
reader, you have permission to mentally picture a very pathetic twenty-
two-year-old me, sitting on the floor and sobbing on the phone to a
complete stranger. I'm certain it was a sight to behold.

Janet: Ma'am? Are you okay? Are you there?
Me: *shakes, sobs, breathes heavily, sniffles*
Janet: Ma'am, may I have your name?
Me: Molly. It's Molly. Buckley. It's Molly Buckley.
Janet: Thank you, Ms. Buckley—
Me: Let me stop you right there. My students call me
    Ms. Buckley. Please call me Molly.
Janet: All right, Molly. Are you okay?
Me: *pauses* No, I'm actually not. Not at all.

---

† There's that hot-chest-feeling again.

Janet: Molly, thank you for your honesty. What's going on today, and how can I help try to make it okay?

I heard it. For a split second, I heard it: compassion. I heard compassion in her voice, and I don't know how or why I felt it, but I did. I began to word-vomit all over Janet (there's the vomit that was missing from the chapter's beginning) and then beg for the overdraft fees to be removed. Janet replied, "Molly, honey, it seems like the overdraft fees are the least of your problems right now. I'll take care of those fees, but it looks like we've got bigger fish to fry. Just exactly how much debt are you in?"

I sighed. "I don't know."

"Okay, honey, we're gonna figure this out," Janet assured me.

For what was easily the next two hours, Janet and I sat on the phone together crunching numbers, going over every bank statement, every bill. When we added it all up, I realized I was over $36,000 in consumer credit-card debt.

The next realization began to wash over me: I only made about $30,000 a year as a first-year high school English teacher. I owed more than I even made in an entire year.

I felt myself slipping back into the panic attack when Janet spoke kindly but firmly, with a tinge of a southern accent, into the phone. "Molly," she said, "you're going to be okay. You are going to get through this. Breathe with me: one, two, three, four . . . Breathe in: one, two, three, four . . . Breathe out . . ."

I was being talked off a ledge by a BB&T customer service representative. And I can only assume that our call was being recorded for quality assurance purposes. Whoever reviewed that call was in for a real doozy.

As I came back down to earth, Janet said, "Molly, this will take work. It won't be easy. But I know you can do it. I have a resource I'm going to connect you with right now—it's called Novadebt, a consumer credit counseling agency—and they help people in situations like yours. I'm going to call them now while you're on the phone, and we'll get you the help you need." (FYI, Novadebt rebranded a few years ago and is now called Navicore Solutions.)

Janet was a woman of her word and stuck it out while she connected me with Novadebt. I was still so overwhelmed, I barely had it in me to bring the representative at Novadebt—let's call her Debbie—up to speed. Debbie had a very, very thick New Jersey accent, and when I balked, Southern Janet stepped in without hesitation and helped fill Debbie in. I'll spare you the nitty-gritty about the next few hours, but once things were handed over to Debbie, she walked me through the process of what getting out of debt was going to look like.

By the day's end, I had a plan.

For what it's worth, and to put things into perspective, had I not gone with something like Novadebt—if I had just cut up all my cards that day and only paid the minimum payment on each one (including interest)—it would have taken me seventy-seven years to pay off my debt. With the debt consolidation plan we created, *including* cutting up all my cards and in addition to the generous reduction of interest rates that Debbie negotiated on my behalf, I could feasibly become debt-free within four and a half years.[‡]

At the very end of the call, Debbie from Jersey asked if she could pray for me. Novadebt, to my knowledge at the time, wasn't a Christian organization, and I certainly wasn't a believer. In fact, I was about as far from God as you could get. By then, not only did I not believe in

---

‡ The difference between debt consolidation and debt settlement is that with debt consolidation, you pay back every cent you owe and, in the end, your credit is basically restored. Debt settlement is not all that dissimilar to bankruptcy; you essentially negotiate a price you'll pay to the creditors, and the rest "goes away" . . . which sounds great, but in the end your credit is often destroyed.

God anymore, but I was so anti-church that even the thought of God made me uneasy. But something told me Debbie was the real deal, so I said yes to her request and she proceeded to pray for me. That prayer was one of the most genuine, kind, heartfelt prayers. Little did I know that her single prayer began to soften the soil in my heart. She was Paul, planting the seeds that would be slowly watered by a cadre of Apolloses over the next two years.

———

When all was said and done, I'd been on the phone for nearly five hours. I'd started the day contemplating suicide but ended the day with the tiniest glimmer of hope.

I felt overwhelmed. I knew this was going to be hard.

When I looked at the final numbers Debbie and I had calculated, my standard monthly expenses would be:

$808 per month toward my debt consolidation payments
$700–$775 per month for rent and utilities (varied depending on the month)
$100 per month for cell phone service
$100 per month for car insurance

My net income as a teacher (after taxes, Social Security, health insurance, retirement savings, etc.) each month was less than $2,000. It was probably more in the neighborhood of $1,800.

I'll state again for the record my incredibly poor math skills, but at the end of the day, after all the basics were met, I had barely $200 dollars to spend on gas, food, and any other unexpected expenses. Let's be real: That's not much.

As panic crept up the back of my neck, I kept hearing Janet's and Debbie's voices in my head, saying, "You can do this. It will take work, but you are capable."

Both of these women were complete strangers, yet they suddenly knew more about me than even my closest friends and family. They had compassion for me, they did not saddle me with shame, guilt, or embarrassment (I was certainly doing enough of that myself), and they sat with me in one of my darkest moments.

I learned a lot from Janet and Debbie that day. I learned that compassion, empathy, and listening go a long way. I learned that oftentimes, people don't need to hear our condemnation for the mistakes they made, but instead our commendation for getting the help they so desperately need. I learned that encouragement, even from strangers, can provide the strength, energy, and emotional stamina to do hard things. I learned that prayer is powerful, and when we offer to pray for someone even when it seems uncomfortable, we could be planting seeds we may never see to harvest. And on the flip side, when we *accept* prayer, it has the power to change hearts. Seeds were definitely sown in my heart that day, though I did not know it at the time.

———

While I felt a glimmer of hope after getting off the phone with Janet and Debbie, I had a sense of foreboding too. I had come to terms with the fact that this was *my* mess of my own making, it was *my* mountain of debt. Not my dad's debt, my sister's debt, or the government's debt—it was *my* debt. And the very real situation I was facing—knowing I no longer had access to a credit card if I was in a pinch and that my monthly expenses were now going to be very, very strict—meant I had to get my life together. I didn't get into debt overnight; I most certainly wasn't going to get out of it overnight.

No one could find out about this.

Not my dad. Not my sister. Not my friends. Definitely not my roommate. What would they think of me? I was convinced that if they knew, they'd judge me, shun me, or disown me.

I was so ashamed, so embarrassed. I'd made my bed and I was going to lie in it. Alone.

Moments later, I heard my roommate walk in the front door. I quickly gathered myself, wiped the tears from my eyes, slapped some powder foundation on my face to hide any remaining splotchiness, and walked out of my room like everything was copacetic.

Abaigh yelled from downstairs, "Mollyyyyyyyy, a couple of us are headed to the Hill Café for dinner and drinks! Wanna go?"

I knew I couldn't go. After the day I'd just had, I couldn't go back to business as usual. I needed an excuse.

"Oh man, I really want to! But I can't tonight . . . I'm not feeling 100 percent and kinda wanna just lie down and read for a while. Have fun without me!"

"Okayyyy fineeeee," she grumbled.

I wallowed in self-pity as I listened to Abaigh, Bennett, Shawn, and Christina jet out the door, laughing on their way to dinner.

How am I going to keep up this charade? I asked myself.

I sat that night trying to itemize every possible expense I had. How on earth was I going to get through the next few years? I knew my income was already a problem that wasn't going to get better on its own, so a logical next step was to figure out ways to make more money.

I went through my room, pulled out every expensive item I owned, and put it into a pile. Every irresponsible purchase I'd made—

designer bags, shoes, books, DVD boxed sets of the shows *Lost* and *24*—anything I knew I could sell.

One by one, I posted the items on eBay to see what I could get for them. RIP to my Louis Vuitton Speedy bag, RIP to my Chanel earrings, RIP to my Theory blazers, RIP to my Thomas Pink boots, RIP to my DVD boxed sets of *Lost* and *24*.[§]

Everything of "value" had to go.

Anything I couldn't sell on eBay, I bagged up to take to Plato's Closet, where some seventeen-year-old proceeded to tell me she could give me only $3.75 for my favorite periwinkle J.Crew sweater.

"That sweater's cashmere! It was over a hundred dollars!"

"I can give you $3.75," she couched as she looked at me with the face of a Tibetan sand fox.

I snatched the cash out of her hand. I took the money because I had to, but I wasn't going to like it or do it nicely.

I began to brainstorm ways to pick up odd jobs. Since I was headed into the summer months as a teacher, I had extra time and figured I might as well use the days off to earn extra money. I had a wide variety of skills . . . Someone would want to pay me to use them, right? Hire me for photography? Check. Hire me for some freelance writing? Check. Pay me to sell some improv shows and corporate team-building workshops? *I've got you.* Bonus: Selling for the improv theater where I performed meant I didn't have to pay for classes—so I was able to keep taking classes and performing without breaking the bank.

———

§ *This was before streaming, okay!?* You had to rent DVDs through the mail . . . and even then you could rent only one or two at a time. Those DVDs were *very difficult things to part with.* Kids these days don't even *know*!

After selling what felt like everything that I owned, after picking up odd jobs, and after cutting out every unnecessary expense—I still couldn't make headway. I was barely scraping by.

The country was heading into a gas crisis in the summer of 2008, and gas prices were over four dollars per gallon. Any extra money I made went toward gas. I had no idea how I was going to pay for food.

One of my lowest points was in the fall of 2008. I was back to work for the semester, and since my days were filled with teaching and coaching, I wasn't able to keep up with my freelance work. I felt like a boa constrictor had wrapped itself around my wallet and was squeezing tighter and tighter.

I had no extra money for food. Novadebt had given me a list of resources in my area if I was ever in a time of need . . . and I knew the time had arrived.

I pulled out a "Food Resources" list and found an organization called Angel Food Ministries. The ministry would, no questions asked, supply groceries to whoever needed them. So that night, I headed to a church nearby and got in line. As I waited for my turn, the shame I felt hung over me like a cloud.

I shouldn't be here.

I don't deserve this food . . .

I got to the front of the line and handed over my empty box. Then the kind volunteers filled the box with groceries, handed it back to me, and said, "God bless you!"

I walked away feeling complete and utter shame. I got to my car and moved the groceries from the box to Harris Teeter bags so that when I got home, my roommate would think I'd gone grocery shopping.

I continued to say no when my friends invited me out to dinner, drinks, or movies. At first they'd ask me if something was going on, but after a while, they stopped asking. The few times I said yes were to Monday wing nights at the bar down the road, where chicken wings were ten cents apiece. Those were the best nights because I could feel somewhat normal, eat a decent meal, and not feel like I'd blown all my money.

When I wasn't working or gorging myself on ten-cent wings, I was at the improv theater rehearsing, practicing, and making people laugh onstage. My best friend Bryan and I were regularly writing and making YouTube videos for our wildly successful comedy news show, *Forget tha Facts*. At its peak, we had twenty-four whole subscribers!

I was, once again, scouring job boards in New York City and calculating somehow, someway to get up to New York and pursue my dream of being on *SNL*.

The facade I'd created—the one that suggested I was killing it in every area of life—was so convincing, I'd almost believed it myself. *Almost.* The reality was, my depression continued to worsen, and I was regularly sinking back into a pattern of suicidal ideation.

When I was alone, I would obsessively flip through my past choices, replaying each one over and over in my head, wishing I'd acted differently. I would get so angry I would yell, scream, cry, and question God, asking him how I'd gotten to this point. I always felt like he was silent, like he wasn't listening, like any semblance of God I'd remotely known had completely abandoned me. Eventually, I reached a point where I no longer believed in God at all. I would regularly mock God and anyone who believed in him, and I completely denied his existence.

I was alone in every sense of the word.

I still had a long way to go. Not only did I have some serious financial messes to fix, but I also had a lot of personal work to do on myself—owning up to my failures, learning from my mistakes, and beginning the healing process.

The problem was, I thought I was going to be able to do those things on my own. No one, no thing, and certainly no God could help me.

It would take a couple of years, but soon I'd learn just how wrong I was.

16

THE BOYFRIEND CHAPTER

1990–2009

> Before you marry a person, you should
> first make them use a computer with slow
> internet to see who they really are.
>
> UNKNOWN

I am often asked why I quit a great job, left my home state of Virginia, and moved to North Carolina with no job lined up at the height of a recession, with basically no friends, and with tens of thousands of dollars in debt. I didn't have a great answer then and, even now, I am not sure I have one. But, at the time, the short answer was so I could further pursue comedy *and* pursue a relationship with the guy I was dating. In retrospect, that was clearly delusional on my part . . . but, for some vital context as we enter this next season on our hero's journey, you first need a small glimpse into the world of my love life. Over the years, my track record for romantic suitors was . . . rocky at best.

My first experience with a "boyfriend" was in kindergarten. His name was Randy and he had a full face of acne and smelled like mung beans. He wore the same McDonald's T-shirt and Puma shorts to school every day (by choice), and early on in our courtship, he told me he wanted to marry me. We would sit together during circle time, and every now and again, his hand would brush against my kneecap. One time, I was whipping up dinner for him in the play kitchen: a slice of pizza, some wooden pears, a plastic cupcake for dessert, and a room-temperature block of juice. He boldly stood beside me while I hovered over the play oven, stylizing his dinner plate, and kissed me on the cheek. It was a truly salacious affair. He "broke up with me" halfway through the school year because "something better came along." We were five.

I was uninterested in getting into a relationship in first and second grades because I was just trying to focus on myself.

By third grade, I had the biggest crush on a boy named Jimmy. He had the most beautiful blue eyes and that early '90s skater boy shag haircut, and he wore JNCO Jeans, band tees, and black Vans. *Vans! Swoon!* But Jimmy was way out of my league. I was still recovering from my mullet years and would sometimes pee myself if I laughed too hard. I had friends, but not many. Jimmy was one of the most popular boys in third grade, and his buddies got wind of my undying love for him, so they *dared* him to ask me out. Jimmy, being the consummate bad boy, was always up for a dare, and so he obliged. When he asked me to be his girlfriend at recess the next day, I stuttered and exclaimed, "Yes!" and immediately ran away from him to tell my friends. That exchange would be, quite literally, our only interaction for the next three days.

When I passed Jimmy walking in the hall, on the playground, or in the lunchroom, I was so terrified to even talk to him that I would run in the opposite direction or just plain hide. I couldn't even say hello. But you bet I told *everyone* that Jimmy was *my* boyfriend. I even told my mom that I had a boyfriend! And we were going to get married! And have babies! And buy a house across the street! "That's nice, sweetheart," Mom said.

Three days later, my best friend Becca learned that Jimmy's pro-posal was actually a dare. I was crushed. Wrecked. Heartbroken. I sobbed on the swings and said to anyone who tried to ask me what was wrong, "I've been *lied to* by the love of my life!" Once he got word that I knew about the dare, he came up to me at recess and said, "This isn't going to work out after all."

I went home from school that day, collapsed into my mom's arms, and cried like a baby. "I will never love again!" I wailed.

My incredible, patient, caring mother held me, stroked my hair, and repeated, "Shh, it's going to be okay. I promise."

I was certain I would be single forever. I was eight.

That heartache led me to have major trust issues with boys. This, coupled with the fact that Mom got sick while I was in fourth grade, meant I had zero time for love interests.

———

By sixth grade, I was ready to open my heart again. Then there was Tony. Oh, Tony. He was tall, dark, and handsome. He had to be eight feet tall. Tony got in trouble a lot, but I liked that about him. I never got in trouble, so I might as well live vicariously through the boys I liked. Tony wore a Grant Hill Detroit Pistons jersey, so naturally, I wore a Grant Hill Detroit Pistons jersey. (Side note: Grant Hill gradu-ated from my rival high school and also went to Duke. I am a Carolina fan. I have no idea why I was into Grant Hill.) In any event, my best friend at the time, Callie, happened to be dating Tony's friend Chris, and so I thought with our one degree of separation, I should shoot my shot. One particular Friday, Callie was spending the night at my house. Since TikTok didn't exist, we did what every other '90s kid did and called Tony on the phone.

"Call Tony and ask him to go steady with you!" Callie demanded.

Because every eleven-year-old in the '90s asked other kids to go steady with them.

I picked up the phone and dialed his number. After talking to *his mom* and asking if Tony was home, he picked up.

Tony: Hello?

Me: Tony, would you like to go steady with me?

Tony: Sure! Do you want to head on down to the li-bary?

Me: Huh?

Tony: You know, the li-bary, so we can study.

Me: No, not study, *steady.* Will you go steady with me?

Tony: Yeah, *when* do you wanna go to the li-bary?

Me: Not study, *STEADY.*

Tony: *Yes, when do you wanna go to the li-bary?*

Me: Ugh, never mind.

Tony: Molly, you needa take a chill pill.

That is, word for word, how that conversation went down. It was like a sixth-grade-romance version of "Who's on First?"

I don't know that you could ever call our relationship a relationship, but we hung out every now and then over the course of a few months. Callie and Tony's friend Chris were also on-again, off-again. One day, Callie said, "Let's sneak Tony and Chris over to your house while your parents are gone!"

"Okay," I said reluctantly, then proceeded to invite them over. Now, my room at the time was on the second floor of the house (I didn't move into the attic until high school), and the tin roof over the porch was right outside my window.

We were hanging out in my room listening to WPGC 95.5, the

top hip-hop and R&B station in Washington, DC, and Callie and Chris sat there French kissing right in front of us. I was in no way going to kiss Tony. Nope. Not going to happen. Not even a chance. Everything about this was so awkward. Even as I sit here recalling these harrowing events nearly thirty years later, I am cringing.

About an hour or so went by, but we lost track of time. Suddenly I heard my parents coming in the front door.

Oh my gosh! My parents are here! They are going to FLIP if they find you guys in my room!

Frantic, I did the only thing I could think to do: kick them out onto the roof. These boys were young and spry, so they could jump off the roof, no problem. I didn't care about the height; I just wanted them out.

The windows in our hundred-year-old home were old, rusted, and nearly impossible to open, but with the strength of She-Hulk, I threw open the window, shoved those boys onto the tin roof, and said, "We'll see ya!"

As I rushed to slam the window shut, part of the glass shattered and cut the far left knuckle on my left hand. It bled everywhere. My parents were so confused. I still have a faint scar on my knuckle to this day.*

I never hung out with Tony again.

In eighth grade, a boy named Logan asked me to the class dance, and I couldn't believe it. Was this another dare?! His dad was the mayor of our town! (Yes, *that* mayor—the one I pestered for years about sidewalks.) Logan was so cute and really popular. He liked Blink-182, and he was, after all, the son of a *famous politician*. I had

---

* I read a draft of this story to my dad, and it was the first time he'd ever heard it. I'd kept the story a secret for nearly thirty years. Needless to say, he was pretty sure he'd known what was going on. He also laughed to the point of tears.

hit the eighth-grade dance date jackpot. He came to pick me up and put a corsage of pink carnations and baby's breath on my wrist. Then we got into the back seat of his mom's gold Chrysler Concorde and rode to the dance, never making eye contact.

If you took every cliché and trope from every middle school dance in the history of middle school dances and boiled it all down to a demi-glace, this dance would have been the end result.

This dance had everything: chocolate fountains; the principal, Mrs. Wintergreen, yelling at kids to "leave room for Jesus!"; horribly posed couples' photos against a blue splattered backdrop; my friend Colleen crying in the bathroom; Lillian's way-older date who was probably a junior in high school; someone's mom . . .

Logan and I alternated between awkwardly standing near each other, splitting up to go talk to our friends, participating in the various dance circles, and stopping by the dessert buffet . . . all until the opening bars of K-Ci & JoJo's "All My Life" came on. Then we made our way toward each other for the pinnacle of the evening: the slow dance.

To this day, I am unable to hear "All My Life" without being transported in my mind's eye to the Herndon Middle School cafeteria or the Herndon Community Center gymnasium.

After the dance, Logan and I went to get milkshakes a couple of times. We went to see *Austin Powers: The Spy Who Shagged Me* at the theater, and he kissed me on the soccer field after school one day. But in mid-June, right at the end of the school year, Logan sent me an email. This was 1999, so email was barely a thing people used—*and yet* he sent me an *email* breaking up with me so he could be single when he went to diabetes camp over the summer. He had type 1 diabetes, and every summer, apparently, diabetes camp was the place to see and be seen. He didn't want to be encumbered by this old ball and chain.

Then there was Kevin. Kevin and I dated on and off from seventh through tenth grade. (It should be noted that we were most definitely in an off period when I went to the eighth-grade dance with Logan.) I cannot even begin to count the number of times we broke up and got back together. We met in our third-period seventh-grade earth sciences class, where he sat behind me all of first semester. He and Colin would play bloody knuckles and get sent to the principal's office regularly. This should have been a clue for me.

Like it was for most American kids, middle school was just awful. My self-esteem was at an all-time low, the friend drama was real, the bullying was real, the puberty was real. All of this, coupled with the fact that I had a very sick mom at home whom I was helping to care for, made for an absolutely miserable couple of years.

So when Kevin started to pass me notes in the middle of class telling me I was pretty, I perked up. I craved positive attention, no matter where it came from.

Kevin was my first real kiss and the first boy I thought I actually loved. But Kevin was also my very first experience with verbal and physical abuse. Soon after we began dating, a darker side of him emerged. He had a host of issues and preyed on my raging insecurities and bouts of depression. I'd heard rumors that he was drinking or doing drugs, but he knew how I felt about those things, so he hid them from me. However, it didn't take long for him to start calling me while drunk or high to berate me over the phone or call me a prude for not doing anything beyond kissing him.

"You've gotten so fat."

"You were prettier when I first met you."

"I wish you had bigger boobs."

"You are so ugly, I don't know why I date you."

"Are you sure you want to eat that? It's probably gonna make you fat."

"You're such a prude. All the other guys I know are having sex."

"You're such an idiot."

He said all this to me on a regular basis.

Kissing him was as far as I wanted to go, but he would often get very physical, grabbing my arm, pushing me, or putting his hands around my neck to threaten me. A few times, I feared he might seriously hurt me.

He would skip school and go off with his buddies to cause all kinds of trouble. One day in particular, he managed to team up with two guys named Ricky and Blaze to go into the sewer system underneath the town square. Why they felt compelled to do this, I have no idea. While they were down there, somehow Ricky's pants caught on fire, and Blaze burned the soles of his shoes. Kevin decided to leave them both behind to fend for themselves. I tell you this story to help illustrate the sheer craziness I'd connected myself to.

Kevin was also a cheater. If I "upset him" because I didn't do what he wanted me to, he would find another girl. It was usually a girl named Rosie, and he would proceed to kiss her right in front of me. Friends warned me to stay away from him, but his master manipulation skills somehow kept me entangled in his web for years.

"I'm so sorry, baby."

"You're the only one I ever loved, baby."

"You're so beautiful, and I'm so terrible, baby."

"Take me back, baby. I'll never do it again."

I was twelve, thirteen, and fourteen years old when this went on.

He broke up with me for the very last time near the end of tenth grade, when I was at one of my lowest points. I saw him walking by in the hallway a few days later. He was clearly high, and he shoved me into a locker and muttered, "Idiot." I am not a fighter by nature and don't think I could ever physically hurt a person, but at that moment, a rage welled up from a place deep inside that has never surfaced again. I grabbed him by the shoulders, slammed him into the locker, and kneed him directly in the twig and berries. I whispered in his ear a phrase about never touching me again, but it happened to include a few choice words I would rather not repeat.

Moments later I looked over to see that my favorite English teacher, Ms. B, had spotted the whole interaction. I thought for sure I was about to be sent to the principal's office. But with compassion in her eyes, she looked at me, winked, and mouthed, "I'm proud of you."

Kevin was kicked out of school the following year, and today he's currently serving a forty-year sentence for first-degree murder. *Actual* murder. During the sentencing, the judge looked at Kevin and said, "There is nothing redeeming about you."

I wanted to title this book *So I Dated a First-Degree Murderer*, but that got shut down.

———

After Kevin, my self-confidence plummeted to new depths. I couldn't believe that a guy would even be interested in me anymore. I had a few boyfriends like Kalid, one of my close friends I'd secretly had a crush on for a while, but he turned out to be in love with my best friend. Then there was Mike from my golf team (the one who I'd gone to Catholic Mass to try to impress) who took me to prom, but he broke up with me too.

Are you exhausted yet? I tell you, the amount of effort I put into my teenage love life is truly something.

And then there was James—the sweet, poor soul one year my junior who asked me to be his girlfriend a mere five days before the death of my mother. *Five days.* He was a good kid, but man, he never had a chance. Remember how he broke up with me at the end of *my* freshman year of college so that *he* could go off to college single? *Rolls eyes* Bless his heart.

In the fall of 2004, the first semester of my sophomore year of college, I met Derek. We had an English class together, and toward the end of the semester, he asked me to come study with him. We'd been flirtatious all semester, and I knew at this point he liked me. We started hanging out pretty regularly, and in January, he asked me to be his girlfriend. We dated for the rest of college, except for a brief breakup for about two weeks during our junior year when he ended it with me because I wouldn't go on a spring break trip with him and all of his friends. Mind you, I'd already gone with him and his guy friends the previous year . . . Why on earth would I want to spend *another* seven days with nine dudes at the beach? Hard pass.

Derek, like me, wasn't perfect by any means, but he was a really good guy, and we had a lot of fun together. His friends were my friends, and I absolutely adored his family. I loved him a lot, but something deep within me knew he wasn't the one for me. I broke up with him at the end of the summer after we graduated in 2007. Our breakup was, by far, the hardest I'd gone through, but I knew it was right and necessary.

For a *host* of reasons, many of which should be blatantly obvious, I spent the next year very much single and not ready to mingle.

My love life thus far had been a train wreck. I'd expend so much effort trying to find my place in a relationship, only to end up with another guy who just wanted to make me his puppet. And the moment I somehow didn't conform to what he wanted, he'd drop me like an old habit.

Deep down, I knew that I was desperate for anything remotely close to what my parents had. Their marriage was, in my mind, what every marriage should look like. I wanted so badly to be loved by someone the way my dad had loved my mom, to be pursued the way my dad pursued my mom. I longed to be accepted the way my dad embraced my mom—flaws and all, in sickness and in health, for richer or for poorer, 'til death would them part.

As I inched closer and closer to rock bottom, my search for that perfect, once-in-a-lifetime love only seemed to act like kerosene on a lit flame. I didn't think it could get worse.

But somehow it did.

Enter: Richard.

17

NORTH CAROLINA

JUNE 2009

Even the darkest night will end and the sun will rise.

LES MISÉRABLES (THE MUSICAL)

Hiding my financial situation from everyone around me became increasingly difficult. Prior to that fateful day in June, I'd already planned and booked three big trips for the summer of 2008. In July, I was chaperoning a field trip to Costa Rica with some teacher friends. Then I was headed to Portland, Oregon, for an improv comedy festival, and to New York City in August for the annual Del Close Marathon—an improv marathon held by the Upright Citizens Brigade Theatre.

While I'd already booked and paid for the flights on credit cards, I hadn't actually taken the trips yet, so I had no idea how I was going to make them work. I sold as much as I could to cover my expenses while I was there, and somehow, by the skin of my teeth, I did it.

I was in such a strange place because I was simultaneously isolating myself, having the time of my life amid once-in-a-lifetime experiences, and sinking deeper into a state of depression thanks to the demons of shame and guilt. Many nights I'd lie in bed and sob myself to sleep.

In late July, I headed to Portland for an improv comedy festival with some improvisers from the comedy theater where I performed in Richmond. The deeper I sank into a depression, the more I poured myself into my comedy. Comedy became a primary coping mechanism. I told myself I was still preparing for a life of stardom on *SNL*.

If I was making people laugh, then clearly I was fine. Right?

I loved going to workshops and learning from some of the best comedians in the country. I loved watching shows and seeing how other improvisers worked—creating a completely made-up show that looked like it was totally scripted. I loved the in-the-moment nature of improv. The adrenaline as I took the stage, awaiting the suggestion of an audience member to guide our scenes . . . It was such a rush.

After each day's workshops and shows, we'd head to the after-party for plenty of dancing, drinking, and debauchery. I'd started talking with a successful comedian named Richard, who was clearly the life of the party. Everyone knew who he was, everyone wanted to talk to him, and everyone wanted to be around him. He had a magnetic personality and a certain *je ne sais quoi*.

We had mutual friends, and before I knew it, he was talking with me at the after-party. He was flirtatious and seemed really interested in me. No one had shown much interest in me in quite a while, so in a plea for attention, I clung to whatever he gave me.

After casually flirting for a while, he asked if I'd go back to his hotel room with him. That was not my style at all, but he seemed so nice, and I wanted to get to know him more. I'll spare you the details, but the next few hours were not some of my prouder moments.

As I left his room and went back to mine, I felt this pit in my stomach. Who was I? Who had I become? I didn't recognize myself.

The next morning, I ran into Richard in the lobby of the hotel. He was talking with some friends and he barely looked my way.

I was so confused.

I felt so low.

As the festival wrapped up and we headed to the airport, I ran into Richard, and this time, he was alone. He came up to me and asked, "Hey, can I have your number?"

That morning I'd barely existed, and now he wanted my number? I reluctantly gave it to him, thinking I wouldn't ever hear from him.

But as soon as I landed in Richmond, I had a text from Richard.

"So, that happened." That was all it said.

"Yeah, I guess it did," I replied.

I had no idea what to make of him. He started texting me more and more, and before long we were texting all throughout the day and even talking on the phone. He was coming up to Richmond the next month and wanted to hang out some more.

Pretty soon, it was clear that we were in a relationship. In the beginning, he would travel from North Carolina up to Richmond to see me a couple of times a month, but every time I brought up the idea of visiting him, he was hesitant. Not until late October did I go there for the first time.

Over the next few months, our relationship grew, and I fell very much in love with him. I thought he was funny, I thought he was charming, he was successful, and he took care of me. It was as if I'd been hypnotized. Whatever he said, I believed. Whatever he did, I wanted to do.

I was a strong, independent woman, but if he said "Jump," I'd say "How high?"

All along, I flat out ignored the red flags.

The first being what he called his "work mode." If Richard was in "work mode," I wasn't supposed to address him or really come near him at all. If he was working at home, I shouldn't bother him. If he was working at the theater, I shouldn't talk to him. If he was talking with improvisers or teaching a class or doing anything remotely related to his job, it became clear that I wasn't to speak to him unless spoken to.

I felt so anxious around him because I was never quite sure if I was allowed to talk to him or not. I was his girlfriend; why couldn't I speak to him? "Because he's busy" was how I managed to justify it.

The second red flag was the number of people who warned me about him. No fewer than seven or eight people on different, separate occasions made comments along the lines of "Molly, you are so nice and such a great person. You can do so much better than Richard. He doesn't treat you the way you should be treated. I like the dude, but you can do way better."

"I think he's changed!" I'd retort.

The third red flag was the way he commented on my food or clothing choices—implying that I was getting fat or he didn't like something about my body. I started to feel like I was being manipulated so that he could get whatever he wanted physically out of me.

But I ignored all those things. I was wearing rose-colored glasses, convinced this was what I deserved and what was best for me.

He knew my dreams of moving to New York and pursuing improv and comedy, but he convinced me that I wasn't cut out for it. "Move to North Carolina! Come live down here. Work with me. I'll make you great," he'd insist.

He knew some details about my financial situation, too, but he definitely didn't know the whole of it. What he did know, he'd find ways to make digs about whenever possible.

After not much convincing, I agreed to move to North Carolina to be closer to him and to study and perform with him. I wasn't going to move in with him but would get my own apartment nearby.

I was leaving my teaching job after just two years, leaving my friends and the place I'd called home, moving to a state with no job lined up and tens of thousands of dollars in debt, knowing only Richard and a few of the people at the theater. Thankfully, my sister and brother-in-law lived about an hour away from where I was moving, so I would at least be closer to them.

That summer, on June 18, 2009, I packed up my place in Richmond; said goodbye to my teaching job, my roommate, and my friends; and moved to Carrboro, North Carolina.

When I got to town, Richard asked me if I wanted to come with him the next morning to do a segment on the local radio station. The theater had a deal with the station to do a comedy news bit, similar to *SNL*'s "Weekend Update," three mornings a week. I loved comedy news writing and was so excited for the opportunity.

The next morning, my first morning in North Carolina, I rolled into the station with Richard to do the segment. I walked into the on-air studio and met John, who worked at the station and was filling in for the regular morning host who was away on vacation. John looked in no way happy to see us and seemed absolutely miserable the entire time we were there. He didn't crack a smile or laugh at a single joke we made. (I would later come to learn that this was because he felt about Richard the way fourteenth-century Europeans felt about the bubonic plague.)

I absolutely loved doing the segment and hoped I'd get the chance to do more.

"You're really great at that," Richard said. "You want to help write these for us and do the segments weekly?"

I couldn't believe it. This was an actual dream come true. For months, I spent Sunday afternoons in writing meetings before going to the station on Monday mornings to record the segments for the week.

I loved writing jokes and developing recurring characters. The morning segment became beloved in much of the Chapel Hill–Carrboro community and a new staple of the morning show radio program.

But while I loved it, it didn't pay anything. I was very much still in debt and very much still without a job. I'd been living in Carrboro for nearly two months, scraping by with what cash I'd had from selling stuff on eBay before I moved. I needed a job. Badly. I applied for nearly a dozen jobs, but nothing was panning out. I got to the final stages of the interview process for a job as a tenth-grade English teacher at the local high school. I thought it was meant to be because the description was identical to the job I'd left—English teacher, photojournalism teacher, and varsity golf coach. I had high hopes, but those hopes were thwarted when I learned the other candidate being considered was a thirty-year teaching veteran who'd been laid off from another district.

She got the job. I didn't.

The "honeymoon phase" of moving to North Carolina to be closer to Richard was over quicker than it started. Within a few months, our relationship felt tense, and he was distant. I finally got a part-time job at a local art gallery and novelty toy store—which I loved because I basically got paid ten dollars an hour to sit at the register and write jokes, develop sketches for the theater, or work on my "budding" blog and YouTube channel with eight subscribers. I also had periodic interactions with Senator John Edwards because his kids loved the store.

While ten dollars an hour was great, it wasn't paying my bills or paying off my debt. I was still doing some freelance work and social media management for people, and I started attending LEADS Group and chamber of commerce meetings to try and drum up more business. When that wasn't happening, I got a food runner and waitress job at a local restaurant in town. When the art gallery and restaurant jobs weren't enough, I picked up a third job working at Anthropologie at the mall.

Then, one morning in early December, I came to the radio station to record our comedy segment. The general manager stopped me and said, "Molly, are you interested in working here? We just had a front desk job become available. We think you'd be a great fit and would love for you to apply."

I applied that day, was interviewed the next, and was hired the week after. It was part-time work paying barely above minimum wage, but working at a radio station felt so cool and provided a lot of opportunities for me to stretch my creative muscles.

By January, I was working four jobs, closing in on 120 hours, seven days a week. I'd work at the art gallery in the morning and the restaurant at night, or I'd work at the radio station in the morning and Anthropologie in the evening. It was as exhausting as you can imagine.

Things with Richard had gotten really bad. He'd become so distant, and I suspected he might be cheating on me. He constantly made excuses as to why he couldn't hang out, and we spent more time arguing than not. The first week of January, he showed up at my apartment and broke up with me.

I was devastated. I knew deep down he wasn't "the one," and I knew he wasn't good for me either. I didn't like who I was with him, and I didn't like who he'd become. I felt so lost. I was living alone in a state where I had very few friends, working four jobs, trying desperately to get out of debt, hiding my secrets from everyone around me, running myself ragged, and performing comedy at a theater where I was bound to see my ex-boyfriend.

That winter and into the spring, I spiraled into an ever-deeper state of depression. As I lay in bed at night, I'd contemplate suicide to the point where I mapped out when and exactly how I'd do it. Then I'd cry even harder thinking about how long it would take someone to find me—how the only reason I'd be missed would be because I hadn't shown up to one of my jobs.

There were nights when I was on the edge of making an irreversible decision, but something inside kept me from going through with it. Something told me to keep going. Something told me to not give up. For the next couple of months, I continued to go through the motions: show up to work, go from one job to the next, put my nose to the ground, and get it done. I worked harder than I'd ever worked on anything. I was desperately trying to make progress, but every time I took one step forward, I'd fall three steps back. I got a speeding ticket on the way to work one day, and the next week, I got in a car accident. The universe was beating me up when I was already down, and I had no clue how to pay for any of it.

By early spring, my coworker John (that guy who hadn't laughed at any of our jokes) had pushed hard for me to move toward full-time work at the radio station. My boss called me into her office and said, "We'd like to bring you on full-time. Would you be interested?"

The pay was low, but it meant I would finally have health insurance and that I could quit at least two of my other jobs. I'd still have to work two jobs for a while, but I said yes on the spot. This kept me going.

I wanted so badly to get myself out of the pit I'd landed in. I hated myself and who I was. I hated what I'd become. I hated feeling the way I felt. I was sick and tired of being sick and tired. I was worn out and desperate for something—anything—to help me.

18

HARVEY WALLBANGER

SPRING AND SUMMER 2010

Comedy is defiance . . . a snort of contempt in
the face of fear and anxiety. Laughing, we create
room for hope to creep back on the inhale.

WILL DURST

On one of my many trips to New York City to take improv and sketch classes, I saw an improviser by the name of Shannon O'Neill perform a one-woman sketch comedy show. It was one of the most incredible things I'd ever seen. For thirty minutes I sat mesmerized at her seamless transitions from character to character, in and out of accents, using a single prop or change in body posture to convey who she was. I think I may have actually mumbled out loud, "I want to do that."

I'd heard that comedians used one-person shows to showcase their talents and unique skills. Then, if they were good enough, and if their show was seen by the right people in the right venue, it could lead to things like commercial acting jobs, interviews, writing gigs for late-night shows like Jimmy Fallon or Conan O'Brien, or even an invitation to audition for *Saturday Night Live*. Many people don't realize that you can't just up and audition for *SNL*; you have to be *invited* to audition. Even then, it's next to impossible to earn a spot. Comedians like Mindy Kaling, Ellie Kemper, Stephen Colbert, and even Jim Carrey all famously auditioned and weren't cast.

When my life was plummeting to rock bottom, I decided to use the little free time and energy I had to focus on the thing I'd dreamt of doing ever since I saw Shannon O'Neill take the stage: I was going to write and perform my very own one-woman sketch comedy show.

In part, I wanted to prove to myself that I could do it. Another part thought this could possibly be my ticket to New York City. I could perform it in Chapel Hill and Richmond and then pitch it to theaters in New York. It was a foolproof plan. Yet another part of me wanted to show Richard what he was missing. I wanted to show him that I *was* good. I *was* talented. I *was* worthy. I *was* capable of doing it and being great.

In what was probably a hasty move, I decided to take the "fake it 'til you make it" approach and said, "Hey Richard, I've got this one-woman show I've written. Do you think I could put it on at the theater this summer?"

"Sure! Do you have a title yet?" he said.

"Nope, but I'll have it to you next week."

I dove headfirst into writing the show and poured every ounce of everything I had into it. I'd sit in my apartment and improvise with myself, practicing different accents, body movements, and character voices to see what I liked and what flowed easily. Had there been some sort of hidden camera planted in my living room, the footage would have compelled someone to do a wellness check on me.

The more I improvised, the more fun I had with it. The characters started to take shape. Most of them were loosely based on real people I knew or had interacted with at some point. I'd had a lot of different jobs over the years in different industries—restaurants, bars, retail, golf courses, beauty spas, a governor's office, and crab shacks . . . Needless to say, I had no shortage of material to work with.

My vision came together quickly. The show would be a slice-of-life. The audience would drop in on a normal night in a regular old corner Irish pub called Seamus Famous Bar. They'd get a glimpse into the lives of the people who frequented the bar and soon realize this night wasn't actually all that normal of a night . . . because a new guy comes in.

I titled the show *Harvey Wallbanger*. The name came from a rarely ordered cocktail. I was a bartender for a brief period, and I remember one night asking a colleague, "What is that bottle of Galliano doing on the top shelf? I don't think I even know what it's for. No one has ever ordered a drink with it."

"The only drink I've ever made with it is a Harvey Wallbanger," she said. "And that was one time. No one ever orders a Harvey Wallbanger. I think that bottle is at least thirty years old, just like all the other bottles of Galliano in America."

The recipe for a Harvey Wallbanger is:

3 parts vodka
1 part Galliano
1 part orange juice
A maraschino cherry (if you like)

For some reason, it made me laugh thinking about bars all over America with thirty-year-old bottles of a yellow liquor called Galliano. Was the Galliano company out of business? Did they hit their jackpot thirty years ago but were struggling to make ends meet now because their liquor was used in only one drink? Who knew?

I stayed up 'til four a.m. one night typing away. The words flowed like honey in summertime, and I got more and more excited as the show took shape. I recruited a couple of improviser friends to come on as directors for the show—to help me hone the characters, block the transitions, tighten up jokes, and bring it all together.

I'd go to my job at the radio station during the day and come home and work for hours on the script. I poured my blood, sweat, and tears into the show. Quite literally. While practicing a potential transition for a couple of characters, I fell one night and scraped my leg on the coffee table. It gushed blood. I also sweat a lot, not only because it was summer in North Carolina but also because it was a lot of work. And then the tears. The more I wrote, the more I understood the angst and pain I was feeling in my own life was manifesting itself on the pages of the script. Every character's flaws, search for identity, and desperate longing for purpose and meaning were not all that far off from my own.

Since it's not likely that you're my dad (unless you are . . . hi, Dad!) or one of the approximately five hundred people who have seen the show, let me introduce you to the characters of *Harvey Wallbanger*.

- **Meet Karen.** I wrote Karen before Karens meant anything to anyone, okay? Karen is our resident straight man, our rock, and our steady beat throughout the show. She's the head bartender at Seamus Famous Bar and has been for quite some time. She's a middle-aged southern woman who definitely needs to get her highlights touched up. She knows all her regulars by name, including their life stories. She's a bit rough around the edges and doesn't take a lot of crap, but she's smart. Karen's never been married. She's just in the same job she's been in for a long, long time and feels like she's stuck. She moved to the big city with dreams of pursuing acting and never made it big.

- **"No-neck" Nancy.** Now that Nancy is an elderly widowed woman, she's living the life of a twenty-three-year-old that she never could have lived before. She's got really bad scoliosis, and it's caused her to slouch so much that her neck is no longer visible. She desperately misses her late husband, Rodney, and spends as much time as possible recounting all the sweet memories they shared. She used to be a cheerleader for the Houston Oilers during the 1960s. After Rodney died, she went back to school to get an associate's degree in philosophy, solely for the purpose of being able to explain anything and everything. She has a thick, grizzled New York accent and sounds like she smoked four packs a day for forty years . . . because she did.

- **Alfi and Peru are life partners.** They met through a missed connections listing on Craigslist. It wasn't even about them, but they were both convinced enough that it was that they met up and fell in love. They'll never get married. Alfi is incredibly boring and likes things like cartography, cutting bonsai trees, and being vegan (no offense to my vegan friends!). While Alfi loves Peru, he's ridiculously quiet and desperately seeks independence. Peru is from Manchester, as in the UK, not New Hampshire. Her parents did a lot of drugs and named her after the country because that's where she was conceived.

- **Gary is your resident conspiracy theorist.** He's got a deep, Bronx-type accent and is absolutely convinced "they're" out to get him. He says it all started when "they" began putting fluoride in the tap water, then when the Dalai Lama became a CIA agent, then when "Clinton killed Vince Foster," and when we definitely did not land on the moon. He also says that if you read any mainstream newspaper or magazine and put together every third letter of every third word, it spells "Satan rides a sleigh." He dares you to try it. He also believes every bottle of Galliano in every bar has a hidden camera planted inside.

- **Then there's Renada.** Renada is a young woman from Long Island. She always wanted to be a cheerleader for the Houston Oilers but wasn't flexible enough, so she will have to settle for the New York Jets. She is a bit promiscuous but desperately wants to love and be loved.

- **Meet Beth.** Beth is always in the bar on karaoke night, she's always drunk, and she always sings the songs incorrectly. She's also always talking about the guy who broke her heart. She has a beautiful singing voice, but the drunker she gets, the more uncouth she becomes. Her first go-round, she sings "I Can't Make You Love Me" and stops halfway through to cuss out her ex. By the time we meet again, Beth is singing Meat Loaf's "I'd Do Anything for Love (But I Won't Do That)" and is a complete wreck. Needless to say, playing Beth was the most fun.

- **DJ 5-hour Energy.** He is the bar's resident DJ who plays all the EDM hits of the late 1990s. No one dances to his music except for . . .

- **Dance floor girl.** She's always the only one on the dance floor and comes to the bar specifically to hear the beats that DJ 5-hour Energy drops. No one knows her name because every time people ask, she yells it so loudly over the music that no one can understand her.

- **The "new guy."** He's a mystery to everyone. He's quiet and unassuming. He walks into a bar full of regulars, sits down, and doesn't order anything for a very long time. By the time he does order, he orders the drink no one ever orders: a Harvey Wallbanger. He never actually speaks.

I spent three months writing and editing the show, six weeks blocking it, and three weeks rehearsing. It was going to be the Friday night headliner at the theater throughout the entire month of July. It was advertised on the radio, in newspapers, and around town. I also found out that the very tough theater critic from the *Indy Week* paper would be there in the front row on opening night to review it.

The show ended up selling out the entire month of July. My co-worker John and the rest of my radio station colleagues all surprised me by coming to the second week's performance. My dad drove up from Florida. Friends from out of state came to see it. Everyone said they loved it. Well, except the tough local theater critic who gave the show mixed reviews and wrote,

> Reportedly, it was Spalding Gray's favorite joke: A skeleton walks into a bar and orders a glass of beer and a mop. If comedian Molly Buckley's brief one-person show, *Harvey Wallbanger*, is a bit more fleshed out than Gray's dry barroom jape, it still burns up a fairly amusing half hour or so answering the question we've all asked ourselves at some point: What *does* it take for a stranger to get a *drink* around here?

I remember on opening night hearing my dad's laughter in the audience. And for a moment, a wave of sadness came over me. *What would Mom think if she were here? Man, I wish she were here. Would I have made her proud? Would she like the show? Would her laughter be louder than everyone else's? Yes, yes it would.*

I snapped back to reality and finished the show to a packed crowd and a standing ovation. I had done it. I'd proven to myself, to Richard, to my family that I could do this. But I still felt . . . empty. When I got back to my apartment after opening night, I sat there alone and cried. I slowly started to realize that the show was just a reflection of me.

Beth was just an overdramatized me . . . singing love songs at karaoke night and really mad at the guy who broke her heart. I was Karen, who thought I'd be stuck doing the same thing for the rest of my life. I was Renada, convinced I would never be loved. I *was* a Harvey Wallbanger. I was always there, but no one really ever needed me or wanted me, for that matter. I was good for only one thing: making people laugh. I had no purpose, and soon, I felt like everyone was just going to forget about me.

19

I BLAME TOBY KEITH

SUMMER 2010

Above everything else I've done, I've always
said I've had more guts than I've got talent.

DOLLY PARTON

After Richard and I broke up, I was in no place to get into another
relationship, nor did I have any desire. I'd basically sworn off dating
and was considering becoming a nun or finding a bunch of hippies and
moving to a commune and learning how to make my own macramé
vests or churn butter.* I repeat: I did not want a relationship.

But I did want friends. Living alone meant that if I wasn't at work
or at the comedy theater, then I would have to actually *try* to interact
with other human beings. Contrary to popular belief, I am actually an
introvert, so I liked living alone. However, that didn't mean I didn't
want to see people at all. I had a couple of friends from the theater,
but it was hard to align our schedules. Plus, I was working so much, it

---

* As of this writing, I have a genuine desire to own a dairy cow and churn my own butter.
My, how the times have changed.

was hard to find time to socialize. Needless to say, the people I worked with were the ones I spent the most time with.

I was really starting to like my coworker John. Not like as in *liiiiike* like, but like as in like. You know what I mean. He was the one who saw potential in me and really pushed for me to get full-time work. Contrary to my first impression from the day I met him, he actually *did* have a personality and a sense of humor.

He was in sales. I was the "front desk girl," which meant I was in marketing, digital media, reception, on-air work, commercial writing, commercial voicing, photography, UNC–Chapel Hill game coverage, and anything else I was needed for. At a small radio station, everyone does a little bit of everything. On one particular day, John and I were assigned to head down to Kenan Memorial Stadium, the football stadium at Carolina, to interview head coach Butch Davis for a radio commercial he was voicing for a charity event. I was so excited because, as a die-hard Browns fan, I had quite the love for Butch. At the time, he was the only coach since the Browns returned to Cleveland in 1999 to take them to the playoffs, and he had been the head coach at Carolina for a couple of years. He was doing a great job, and I was going to get to meet him!

John came to pick me up at my apartment, and we headed to the stadium. I rambled on and on about how nervous I was, why I was a Browns fan, what questions we'd ask Butch, what his office was going to be like . . . all of that. John just listened and smirked as I rambled. We pulled into Kenan and headed up to the coaches' wing, got buzzed through the doors, and waited in the reception area for Butch's assistant to let us in. John is a Tar Heel, born and bred. He went to Carolina, his parents went to Carolina, and he was—and is—a devoted fan. He loves Carolina football. A lot. But did he geek out like me? Absolutely not. He kept his cool.

We finally got brought back to Butch's office, and I was in heaven. This office was *niiiiiice*. Obviously, it had Tar Heel memorabilia everywhere, a beautiful ornate wooden desk, and really fancy chairs that bounced a little when you sat in them. John and I sat there looking around, and I noticed a big sign that said "COFFEE" taped to the doorframe of the office.

When John saw the sign, he got really excited. I didn't understand why. He explained that Butch was well-known as a great recruiter, considered by some to be one of the best recruiters in college football. And every time news broke of a new high school star committing to play for Carolina, an endless exchange of texts, Facebook posts, and message board discussions would fly among fans lauding Butch's skill as a closer.

"Coffee's for closers only," they'd say, quoting Alec Baldwin's iconic line from *Glengarry Glen Ross*. "Always be closing. Butch is always closing."

Was Butch in on it? Was this his way of reminding himself, every time he left his office, that he should always be closing?

When Butch walked in, John excitedly pointed to the coffee sign and asked, "Always be closing?"

Butch looked at him with a blank stare. "Excuse me?"

"Always be closing? 'Coffee's for closers'? Is that sign a reminder to always be closing new recruits?" John asked.

Butch suddenly looked sheepish. "Oh, no, that's something else." He clearly didn't want to talk about it.

John and I finished recording, and Butch had to rush out for a meeting. So we stuck our heads into his assistant's office and asked about the meaning of the coffee sign.

She exclaimed, with great exasperation, "He keeps forgetting to turn off the coffeepot before he leaves the office. He's ruined three pots, and it's killing me. I put that sign up as a reminder for him to turn it off!"

We both laughed so hard on our way out of the office and back to John's car. We spent the entire ride home talking about it and how Butch probably thought we were idiots, but we couldn't stop laughing.

When John was dropping me off back at my apartment, I looked at him and said, "Thanks, that was actually really fun. See you later!"

It was the first time he'd started to make the shift in my mind from "the stoic guy I work with" to "he's pretty cool. I like this dude. I think we can be friends."

———

A few months later, we were assigned to do a remote broadcast at a local business called Summerwind Pools and Spas. Remotes were a way for advertisers on the radio station to get additional exposure by having us do a broadcast live from their location. I was in charge of photography and social media content for the remote, and John and our coworkers Aubrey and Christy were there to help. John had jokingly said at one point that he would grab a microphone and jump in the hot tub in his swim trunks to broadcast live from the spa.

Maybe I should clarify: I *thought* he was joking. He wasn't actually joking.

Several times an hour, the studio would toss the broadcast to us at Summerwind. We'd go live on the air for three to four minutes, and each time, we'd have to come up with something new and exciting to talk about. We interviewed the owner, we talked about upcoming specials and the different products that Summerwind offered. We were approaching summer season, after all! During the segments, I took pictures and shared them to the radio station's social media accounts.

About an hour and a half into the broadcast, John disappeared into the bathroom and came back out in his work attire with a towel around his neck. I looked at him, puzzled, and said, "What are you doing?"

"Next break, I'm going to get in the hot tub and do a live, on-air product review," he said.

The next thing I knew, he was headed toward a deluxe eight-seater hot tub in the back of the store, towel around his neck, microphone in hand. He proceeded to remove his shirt, drop trou down to his swim trunks, and step into the tub.

You know how whenever a character from *Looney Tunes* spots a looker, his eyes pop out of his head and he howls, "*AWOOOOOOGA*"?

That was me.

For those who are interested or curious and would like me to paint a mental picture for you, let's just say, my colleague was a lot more sculpted than I had anticipated. Pants and shirts were a lot baggier in those days. Picture Jim Halpert's attire in the early days of *The Office*. Now picture John Krasinski's chiseled physique in his *Jack Ryan* era. I did not have a clue that *that* was going on underneath all that late-aughts bagginess.

I looked over at my fellow colleagues. Then we all looked at each other, looked away, and blinked a few times. Christy said, "Oh, come on, pick your jaws up off the floor, we all know John Stillman works out."

The broadcast happened. I took some photos. I cannot confirm or deny if I took a few for my own personal catalog.[†]

I would be lying to you if I said I didn't suddenly have a crush on

---

[†] Look, I'm not saying my behavior at the time was classy, nor would I encourage such behavior of young, single women . . . but I did have eyes. Also, spoiler alert, I'm married to him now, so it all worked out.

John. I still, absolutely, *in no way*, wanted to be in a relationship. But just because I was on a diet didn't mean I couldn't still look at the menu.

He was smart. He was funny. He had a really strong work ethic. He was, for sure, good-looking. He checked a lot of boxes. Why couldn't we be friends? Pals? Amigos?

A month went by, and I was trying to find ways to hang out with John outside of work. We were spending more time together *during* work because we were frequently assigned to the same remotes or events. We both had to cover the Chapel Hill Fourth of July fireworks celebration, and I thought, *Maybe this is my chance . . . We can hang out after the fireworks!*

As we were leaving, I turned to him and said, "Hey, whatcha doing after the fireworks?"

"Oh, I'm gonna go hang out with my friend Casey who is in town," he replied.

Suddenly I was jealous of some chick named Casey. Why was I jealous? I didn't want a boyfriend. I just . . . wanted to hang out. But still, I wanted to know who this girl was. What did she have that I didn't? She was from out of town, so was this a long-distance relationship? Why had he never mentioned her before? *I wonder if I can find a picture on Facebook to see what I'm dealing with here . . .*

Later that week, I learned that Casey was actually a guy, one of his best friends from college.

The next week, I was driving into work, listening to country radio, and heard an announcement that lawn seats for the Toby Keith concert that weekend were ten dollars. *This is my chance!* I thought. *I'll ask him if he wants to go to the concert with me!*

I got to my desk that morning and waited for John to walk in.

"Hey, John! Did you hear? They have a ten-dollar ticket special on lawn seats for Toby Keith this Saturday night!" I said, dropping hints.

"Sweet, really?" he said.

The next thing I knew, he was texting *all of his friends*, inviting *them* to go to Toby on Saturday. My plan was rapidly backfiring.

"Well, if your friends can't go and you need anyone to go with, I'd go with you," I said slyly.

"You wanna go?" He seemed surprised. "You can come with us! I think there are eight guys going!"

Great, I thought. *Fantastic. Me and John and eight of his friends. My plan is flawless.*

Not.

I'd done the "only girl hanging out with a bunch of dudes" thing, and it was not my favorite. But I relented because I wanted to hang out with him, and I really loved Toby Keith.

The Friday night before the concert was the second week of my *Harvey Wallbanger* run, and I had asked all week if John and any of my coworkers were planning to come. They all gave me nonanswers, so I assumed they weren't coming—but to my surprise, they all showed up and packed the house for me. After the show, I stood at the door to the theater thanking people as they were leaving. John came up to me, hugged me, and said, "That was awesome. Great job. See you tomorrow?"

"Yep, I'll see you tomorrow!" I said nervously.

Toby Day came, and I was stressing out about what to wear. If you're a woman, you understand the stress and overthinking that can go into what to wear on a first date. Okay, this wasn't exactly a date, but I still wanted to make a good impression. I wanted to look cute, but not like I was trying too hard. I also didn't want to look frumpy. *This was very difficult.*

I settled on white shorts, a black ruffled top, and my trusty old black cowboy boots. It was a country concert, after all. I drove to his house, and we got in his truck to meet his eight friends in the parking lot of Bojangles. What a great start.

We all piled in a couple of vehicles and headed to the venue's tailgating area. We hung out for an hour or so before the concert, laughing, talking, and eating all the Bojangles tailgate specials. Flirtation was definitely happening between John and me. It wasn't overt, but it was there. I actually really liked his friends, and we were having a great time.

We went into the concert, and he stood by me the whole time. Our arms would brush against each other, or his hand would brush against my back. There was a tension between us I had no idea what to do with.

Was I reading too much into this?

Was he actually flirting with me?

I did *not* want a boyfriend.

As the concert went on, we had arms around each other singing at the top of our lungs to "American Ride," "As Good as I Once Was," and "Courtesy of the Red, White and Blue."

The concert ended, we headed back to the car, and we got in his truck to head home. We stopped at the gas station to fill up, and as I sat in the passenger's seat waiting for him to finish pumping the gas, he came around to my side of the truck, opened the door, and planted a kiss right on me.

I was surprised, but I definitely wasn't complaining.

He looked at me and smiled. "I had a lot of fun with you."

"Yeah, me too. Thanks for letting me tag along," I said.

"Anytime," he replied.

He held my hand as we drove home, and a million thoughts ran through my mind.

What is happening? Is he going to call me tomorrow? He's definitely not going to call me tomorrow, is he? Is it going to be awkward at work? It's going to be awkward at work, isn't it? I do not want a boyfriend. Does he think I want a boyfriend? What am I doing?

I barely slept that night.

The next morning, I woke up, looked at my phone, and saw a text from John.

"Good morning. Are you as good once as you ever was?"

"I think I am, but things can change," I replied.

"Naturally," he said.

WE WERE TEXT FLIRTING.

Okay, breathe, Molly. He actually *texted you. Step one. Now you have to get through step two: work on Monday.*

I got to my desk early on Monday because I didn't want to walk into work *after* him. Somehow I thought that would make it less weird. He walked in about thirty minutes after I got there, and strangely, it wasn't weird at all.

He winked. "Hey."

"Hey yourself," I replied.

Progress. We were making progress.

There was something really easy about this. Again, your girl did *not* want a relationship, so I had nothing to lose. It was fun trying to find ways to hang out. A couple of days later, we were at a chamber of commerce networking event, and he made a passing reference to dollar taco night at the Mexican restaurant downtown.

"Oh, yeah?" I asked. "We should get some of those sometime."

"Like tonight?" he asked.

"Yep," I said.

And off we went. We sat at dinner for over two hours, and the conversation flowed so easily. He drove me home and kissed me in his truck again. "I'll see you tomorrow," he said.

For the next few weeks, we texted each other nonstop, finding any excuse to eat lunch or spend time together. The more I got to know him, the more I liked him. Something about him was different. He wasn't like any other guy I'd ever met. I learned he'd *never* had a girlfriend before (which was great, because I did *not* want a boyfriend!). He told me all about his family and his childhood. He was really open about his faith, and I learned he was a Christian and had been his whole life. A part of me was a bit leery of his faith because of my past experiences, but he was so genuine, so different . . . He seemed to actually walk out what he believed, not just *talk* about it.

We kept what we were doing a secret at work because, you know, it wasn't a thing, so . . . why tell others? That said, I bet everyone else knew and we were just oblivious to their knowledge.

About a month or so later, after we covered a fall fest event at UNC for the radio station, he took me to dinner at Spanky's in downtown Chapel Hill. We sat at dinner for close to three hours, talking about everything. He opened up and told me things he'd never told anyone. We laughed. I cried a little bit. I started to really talk about my struggles, a little bit about my financial situation, and about the death of my mom. The more I spoke, the more he asked. There was never an ounce of shame in his voice, just genuine concern.

As I started telling him about my mom's time in Vietnam and her book, he had this inquisitive look on his face. Then he stopped me. "Your mom wrote a book? About her time in Vietnam?"

"Yeah," I replied.

"Did she go back to Vietnam at the end of the book?" he asked.

"Yes, why?"

"What's the book called?" he continued.

"*Home Before Morning.*"

"No way," he said in disbelief. "I read your mom's book my junior year of college for my American history class. I don't remember a lot of what I read in college, but I remember her book."

"You're joking," I said.

"Nope, not joking," he insisted.

"I can't believe this." I started to tear up. "That is crazy."

"Maybe it's not *that* crazy," he replied. "Maybe I was supposed to read her book so this moment would happen. I don't think it's an accident."

We looked each other in the eyes without saying anything for the next few moments. A feeling washed over us that this, whatever this was, might be different.

But I didn't want a boyfriend. And he'd never had a girlfriend. We weren't boyfriend and girlfriend. So what was *this*, exactly? What were we? What was happening?

20

NEW HOPE

FALL 2010-SUMMER 2011

Imagine a woman who has ten coins and loses one.
Won't she light a lamp and scour the house, looking
in every nook and cranny until she finds it? And when
she finds it you can be sure she'll call her friends
and neighbors: "Celebrate with me! I found my lost
coin!" Count on it—that's the kind of party God's
angels throw every time one lost soul turns to God.

LUKE 15:8-10 MSG

If we look at the culture around us and all the self-help books on the shelves, it would be easy to assume that, if we are lost, we are somehow supposed to find ourselves. I know firsthand that this concept is absolute garbage. I spent basically the first twenty-five years of my life attempting this very thing, only to find myself broke and broken. I knew I was lost, so I did everything in my power to "find myself"—but none of it worked. I was left feeling empty and helpless.

As I mentioned, I knew right away something about John was different. He had this thing about him that I couldn't really put my finger on. Not only did he seem to have his life together, but he also had a confidence about him that made me curious. It wasn't arrogance (although he would joke that that was it). It was a self-assuredness and a lack of caring about what others thought that very clearly came from a foundational faith and an identity in Jesus.

I'd never met anyone like him before.

His birthday was toward the end of September, and his parents were coming to town for the weekend. He hadn't even admitted I was his girlfriend yet, but there he was, asking me to go to dinner with him and his parents that Saturday night. No pressure.

As we sat on my couch talking about our plans, he mentioned in passing that he was going to check out a church called New Hope that Sunday, which happened to be his birthday. He'd gone to New Hope in college but hadn't visited in a few years. He'd been going to a different church with his roommates.

Without even hesitating, I blurted out, "Can I go with you?"

I had no idea where it came from. I'd not stepped foot in a church in *years*. I'd said I didn't even believe in God, and I'd mocked people who called themselves Christians. I was the *last* person who would visit a church willingly. What on earth was I thinking? This wasn't to impress John. This wasn't because I thought he'd like me more if I went. This wasn't about impressing his parents. This came from a place deep inside me—a still small voice that said, *Molly. Go.*

So I asked him again. "I mean, is it *okay* if I go with you to church?"

John looked at me maybe a little bit shocked and said, "Um, yeah, of course you can."

"Great!" I replied.

"I don't have to dress up for this, though . . . right?" I said hesitantly.

"Ha! No, no you don't," he chuckled.

I immediately started questioning why I'd asked him. No church existed that would welcome me. Why would a church want someone like me to walk through its doors—someone who didn't believe what they believed? I was too much of a mess. Wouldn't they sense that and tell me I wasn't allowed in?

I had no idea, but I figured I had nothing to lose. So I was going.

The next morning, John came to my apartment to pick me up. I didn't say a word in the car the entire way, *an obvious rarity for me.* My skin felt hot. I was shaking. I had butterflies in my stomach, and not the good kind.

This was a mistake. We should just turn the truck around right now.

As we pulled into the parking lot, my anxiety rose. But it soon began to ease as we were greeted with smiles and welcomes from every which way.

This is a scam, I thought. *These people don't mean this. Once they find out who I am, they'll turn their backs.*

We found John's friends, David and Kristin, and sat down with them. As the service started, the lights dimmed. The worship team came out, and the music began to play. I loved the music, and this immediate sense of peace came over me. Sure, the songs reminded me of my days as a budding lead singer in a *very* popular midnineties worship band called Doubting Thomas. But in reality, a genuine spirit of humility and authenticity seemed to ooze from each person singing and playing. I didn't know any of the words to any of the songs, but as I listened, something started to shift in me.

Once worship was over, the pastor came out and started talking about the day's service. "Today is a unique day, church!" he said. "Instead of a normal sermon like most Sundays, we have a special guest with us. Tyler Zeller from the UNC–Chapel Hill basketball team is here, and we're going to sit down and have a conversation. Everyone welcome Tyler to the stage!"

The church started applauding as Tyler stepped foot onstage. I was a huge UNC fan and loved Tyler. I had been working at the radio station for almost a year at that point, and covering the games was one of my favorite parts of the job. Tyler's seven-foot stature was hard to miss. He towered over the pastor, literally head and shoulders, as they smiled and shook hands.

The first few moments of the interview were the regular banter about basketball and the season, plus jokes about how the gospel was clearly at work since the pastor was a Duke graduate. Only with God's blessing could a Duke guy and a Carolina guy sit down and have a civil conversation.

But quickly, the conversation got much deeper. I was certainly enjoying it all because, again, any Carolina-blue-blooded Tar Heel fan would. Then the pastor asked Tyler a question: "You were raised in a Christian home and you're still a strong believer. How do you keep your faith at the forefront when it could be so easy in the environment you're in to chase the fame, money, sex, and glory of self?"

Tyler responded earnestly. "My purpose is to glorify God in anything and everything I do. I keep my eyes fixed on Jesus knowing he's the thing that won't fail me when money, power, and fame will." Tyler talked about his identity as a follower of Christ—not as a star player or a Tar Heel or as a man with NBA aspirations.

He went on to describe his love of Jesus, what Jesus did for him, and the reasons for his faith. He talked about the sacrificial love of Christ. He spoke of the finished work of Christ on the cross and how God's love is more powerful than anything. He spoke of repentance and forgiveness of sin.

I realized, in that moment, that this conversation was the very first time in my entire life that I'd ever really, truly heard the gospel articulated.

I'd been around Christians, I'd been to Awana, *I'd been the co-lead singer of Doubting Thomas*, but I'd never heard the foundational gospel message shared so simply and purely. It might seem silly, but as I sat there, I couldn't help but think about how much I wanted what Tyler had. What John had. What the people worshipping around me had.

It had never occurred to me that there really *was* a God in heaven who sent his one and only son, Jesus, down to earth in the form of human flesh. To live a perfect, sinless life. To show us, to show *me* the way of humility, love, mercy, grace, and truth. That the plan all along was that he would be persecuted, tried, and executed on a cross. That he would die a criminal's death and be buried in a rich man's tomb. That he would take on the punishment for our sins, for *my* sins. That his forgiveness was for us, for *me*. But that wouldn't be the end. Three days later, Jesus would rise from the dead—conquering death once and for all—so that we could have eternal life with him forever.

For so long I thought my sole purpose in life was to make people laugh. I thought I was good for nothing else. But I left church that day with a glimmer of hope—that maybe I was still breathing because God wasn't done with me after all. At no moment did I raise my hand and say I was saved. There was no uttering of a prayer accepting Jesus into my heart. There was simply a quiet, private moment between me and God where I said, *Okay, God, I'm here. I hear you. Speak, because I'm listening.*

I had denied God's existence for so long, and now he was standing there staring me straight in the face. I couldn't run any longer.

At lunch after church that day, I asked John if I could go back with him the next Sunday and the Sunday after that. He was excited that I was excited. I looked forward to Sunday each week. The worship experience and the messages were unlike anything I'd ever experienced.

About the fourth Sunday I'd been attending, the pastor started talking about money in his message. "This isn't a popular topic in the church for a lot of reasons," he said. "Money conversations make people uncomfortable, but today we're going to tackle this. Money and possessions are the second-most referenced topic in all of Scripture! There are more than 2,300 verses in the Bible talking about money, and nearly 40 percent of Jesus' parables were about money." He continued, "This message isn't about me wanting something *from* you, it's about me wanting something *for* you."

For the next forty-five minutes, it was as if the message had been written, word for word, for me. Yes, I know this is an incredibly self-centered way to think of it, but hey, I was a baby believer at the time. The message spoke to my every insecurity and view about money. He talked about the biblical tithe—giving 10 percent of one's income back to God. I had been in church before, but I had never in my entire life even heard of a tithe. This was a completely foreign concept to me.

The pastor quoted scriptures such as:

- "'Bring the whole tithe into the storehouse, that there may be food in my house. Test me in this,' says the LORD Almighty, 'and see if I will not throw open the floodgates of heaven and pour out so much blessing that there will not be room enough to store it'" (Malachi 3:10).
- "Remember this: Whoever sows sparingly will also reap sparingly, and whoever sows generously will also reap generously. Each of you should give what you have decided in your heart to give, not reluctantly or under compulsion, for God loves a cheerful giver" (2 Corinthians 9:6–7).
- "Be sure to set aside a tenth of all that your fields produce each year. Eat the tithe of your grain, new wine and olive oil, and the firstborn of your herds and flocks in the presence of the LORD

your God at the place he will choose as a dwelling for his Name, so that you may learn to revere the LORD your God always" (Deuteronomy 14:22–23).

- "Again I tell you, it is easier for a camel to go through the eye of a needle than for someone who is rich to enter the kingdom of God" (Matthew 19:24).

As I sat there and soaked it all in, I was overwhelmed. The message wasn't coming from a place of greed or coercion. It was just a simple explanation of how one should look at finances from a biblical perspective. It was about being a good steward of the financial resources we've been entrusted with—something I'd done a downright pitiful job of.

Here I was, tens of thousands of dollars in debt, barely able to make ends meet. I hadn't been a good steward of anything I'd been entrusted with.

Sitting in the chair in the sanctuary that day, in the only way I can possibly explain it, I heard that still small voice of the Lord, saying, "Test me, Molly. Test me in this area and see if I will not throw open the floodgates of heaven for you. Stop white-knuckling your wallet, because it's got a grip on your heart, mind, and soul."

I thought, *I think I'm supposed to start tithing.*

Right on cue, like in the cartoons with the angel and the devil on each shoulder, I heard that other voice of the Enemy, whispering, "Lies. You're in debt. You can barely pay your rent. How in the world are you going to *tithe*? Don't do it."

I left church that day feeling my soul wrestling against itself. I'd been hiding my financial struggles for so long. I'd been doing all I could in *my* power to get myself out of the mess I'd made. Who was I to think that God was going to somehow get me out of it?

I decided I would take the week to pray about it. This wasn't an approach I'd ever taken before, so I figured, Why not try now? What did I have to lose? After I prayed about it, I decided I would *kind of* give it a shot. The next Sunday, I brought with me a check for fifty dollars. A handwritten check. No, fifty dollars wasn't a full 10 percent tithe, but it was a baby step for me. You have to remember, I was still in a ton of debt working a full-time job that barely paid the bills. Fifty dollars was no small chunk of change to me.

I continued to dive headfirst into church involvement. John and I went to the membership meeting, and I joined right away. I signed up to audition for the worship team and started serving. I had missed singing so much, and it felt amazing to be using one of my gifts in a way that wasn't self-serving.

The status quo for over two years had been about doing things "my way"—and it hadn't worked. I knew it was time to really, truly hand my life over to Jesus.

Two weeks after I gave that first fifty-dollar quasi-tithe check, I got a package in the mail. Inside was a book called *The Blessed Life* by Robert Morris, and with it was a handwritten note:

Molly,

The Lord laid it on my heart this week to send you this book. I pray that it blesses you as much as it has me.

Pastor B

When I asked John if he'd gotten a copy of the book in the mail, he said no. I asked a couple of new friends at church if they'd received the book, and they said no too. I thought, *Well, this is kinda strange, but I'll check it out.*

I opened up the book, started reading, and couldn't put it down. If I'm being honest, the whole concept and idea of it weirded me out.

I mean, the book had absolutely crazy stories. It talked about people who doubled their income in a year after deciding to tithe more generously. Relationships that were once lost were restored. People prayed for a specific need, and that need was fulfilled. No, this book was clearly not some "get rich quick" scheme or anything like that. It was simply one man's testimony of God's faithfulness—stories of total surrender and of what God can do when we realize that everything we have is his to begin with.

My heart posture continued to shift. Something told me to just give it over to God. I had my own little "come to Jesus" meeting with myself and said, "All right, Lord. I've been trying to do things my way for quite some time, and it ain't working. So, *FINE.* I'm going to try it your way. I'll do this. I will tithe. I'm not going to question it, and I'm not going to grumble about it. I'm going to tithe cheerfully."

But the problem was, I had no idea how to make it work. I knew I couldn't figure it out alone. John and I were getting pretty serious by then. He'd *finally* admitted I was his girlfriend when we dressed up as Forrest Gump and Jenny on Halloween. Four days later, he'd told me he loved me. He'd been the one I'd been longing for all along, but he came around when I wasn't looking for him.

I was afraid. While I'd told John about my inheritance and my financial trouble, he didn't know *how* bad it really was—only the high-level, need-to-know information. But I knew I needed to tell him everything.

On a Saturday night in early December, I sat down with him, looked him in the eye, and said, "I have to tell you something. I haven't told you everything about my financial situation or how I got into this mess, but it's time. I want to surrender all of this to God, and I want to start tithing, but I can't figure out how to do it. I need your help, but I'm afraid that once you see it all, you're going to run for the hills—and if you do, I will understand."

I got out all my bank statements, my Novadebt paperwork, my debt payoff schedule . . . all of it. I showed him my income and my expenses. I laid it all out. I was sure he was done.

But he didn't run.

Instead, he grabbed his laptop, opened up an Excel spreadsheet (the guy *loves* spreadsheets), and said, "Let's figure this out."

"I don't want this to be your burden. This is my mess and my problem," I said through tears.

"Well," he sighed, "I want to marry you someday. So it will eventually be my problem. Might as well be my problem now."

After he helped me create a budget and we crunched all the numbers, he saw there was no way I would have enough money to eat *and* tithe. It was one or the other.

John had been in church nearly every Sunday of his life, and he'd always been a faithful giver. But even he was like, "Uh, yeah, I have no idea how you're going to do this. The math just isn't mathing."

"I have to do this, John," I insisted. "My wallet has held a vise grip on my soul for too long. Something has to change. I know this is what I'm supposed to do."

"Well, okay then," he replied. "I'll make you a deal. If you commit to the tithe for the next thirty days, I will buy your groceries. It ain't gonna be prime rib and lobster tails, but I'll make sure you eat. You do what you need to do, and I'll take care of your food."

As he spoke, I felt this tension of embarrassment, shame, humility, and gratitude. I couldn't believe I'd stumbled backward into a relationship with someone who cared so deeply for me and, more importantly, prioritized my relationship with the Lord and was going to do whatever he could to help. At the same time, I felt such shame that I'd gotten myself into this position. None of this was anyone's fault but my own.

So I started tithing. First on my net income, because that was all I could muster, but I was stepping out in faith. The second my paycheck hit my bank account, I wrote out a check for exactly 10 percent of my take-home pay and put it in the basket on Sunday at church. I had no idea how I would find the space in my budget to tithe, but I trusted God to make it happen. I believed he would provide.

In the meantime, I started reaching out to people from the past. I'd fractured some relationships while dealing with my mess, such as with my best friend and roommate from college, Jane Berry. She had eloped to Las Vegas in the spring (yes, they were married by Elvis— very on-brand for her), and they'd decided to have a reception with friends a few months later. I had promised her I would be there, but the day before I was scheduled to drive up for the party, I realized I didn't have enough money to get myself there. Plus, my job had asked me to work late for overtime pay, and I needed the money so badly. Too ashamed to ask for help, I canceled on my friend at the last minute and didn't celebrate with her. This wasn't the first time I'd done something like this. Shame kept me from being honest, and in turn, my friend was hurt and angry. I had screwed up.

Once I had the chance to understand the hurt and pain I'd caused, I knew I couldn't make excuses; I needed to repair the relationship. I reached out and asked if I could come visit her, and if she wanted to see Dave Matthews Band with me in Charlottesville. Dave was our favorite and we'd spent many a late night jamming out in our apartment in college. She agreed, and I went up to meet her. That night at dinner, I looked her in the eye and said, "JB, I'm so sorry, man. I was a terrible friend, I made so many mistakes, I pulled away from you and from everyone else around me, and I pray you can forgive me."

With the kindest and most sincere look, her smile beaming at me, her platinum blond curls bouncing, she replied, "Of course I forgive you. I love you, man." We cried, hugged, ate chips and salsa, and began the process of restoring that which was broken.

———

I was learning that finding real healing in Jesus was so much more than just a singular moment of prayer and saying the words "I believe." Healing includes a slow, necessary, often painful process of sanctification, growth, and change. I was starting to see how the surrender of my wallet was leading to a complete surrender of my heart and mind too.

Then, in January 2011, I got my first bonus, *ever*, at work. The amount was exactly 10 percent of what I took home on a monthly basis. Down to the penny. A little buffer room had appeared in my budget. I tithed 10 percent of that bonus.

Then, in April, I decided to take it a step further: I began tithing on *gross* income instead of net. I was going all in.

Each month, the math would somehow work out, and I'd have exactly the amount needed to get by.

On May 2, 2011, I got an even bigger bonus *and* a raise at my job. From that, I was able to pay off a little more debt. And I realized the belt around my budget was feeling just a little bit looser.

Then I started going above and beyond my tithe. I started giving any chance I could—not because I felt like I had to but because I *wanted* to. "Each of you should *give what you have decided in your heart to give, not reluctantly or under compulsion*, for God loves a cheerful giver" (2 Corinthians 9:7, emphasis mine).

Around this time, I decided I wanted to go on a mission trip to Kenya. I had no clue how to raise $3,500 to go, but I was going to make it happen.

Two weeks before I left for Kenya, I was a thousand dollars short of what I needed. I was panicking.

I was at a business lunch that week with a guy by the name of Gary and his business partner, Sara. Gary owned a large digital media company that specialized in covering the professional audio/visual (AV) industry. He was a devoted listener of the radio station, and he really liked the work I'd been doing. The previous fall, the radio station had promoted me to marketing director,* and I'd been tasked with overhauling the station's digital media presence. The 5000-watt AM radio station hadn't had a new website in close to a decade or been very active on social media, and I really wanted to make the station *the* news source for the Chapel Hill–Carrboro community. I had the idea of rebranding the website to chapelboro.com—and creating a large, community, online hub that would reach well beyond our area.

As we chatted about media, work, and life, they asked me about my upcoming trip to Kenya. I hadn't mentioned *anything* about needing donations or the fact that I was in danger of not going. At the end of the lunch, Gary handed me a check for $1,000 toward my trip.

Once again, it was the exact amount I needed. He did it again. God provided when I needed him to.

I got home from Kenya in early August, and a couple weeks later, Gary and Sara took me out to lunch again. At the lunch, they handed me an offer letter for a digital media job at their firm—a job I had not applied for. A job I had not asked for. A job I had no idea I was being considered for. The position had a ton of growth potential, and it seemed like one I would do really well in. I knew it would be a challenge, but I was ready and excited to take it on.

But as I read the offer letter, my eyes landed on the starting salary.

---

* I got to create my own title—so I chose "Duchess of Digital Media" because that's way more fun to put in an email signature than "Marketing Director."

The job was going to pay me a salary that was exactly—to the penny—double the salary I'd made one year prior. The starting date was a year, to the date, after I started tithing.

As I took it all in, I realized what was happening. There it was—that still small voice in my head, clear as day, saying, "I told you if you tested me that I would provide."

I sat down on the curb outside my office and broke down. I was wrecked.

I hadn't by any means "arrived," but my small steps of faith had led me right to the feet of the One who had been there all along.

21

GREEN ACRES

SUMMER 2011–PRESENT

Therefore, if anyone is in Christ, the new creation
has come: The old has gone, the new is here!

2 CORINTHIANS 5:17

After more than a decade of walking with Jesus, I have had many
a conversation with people about how they came to faith. Many,
like my husband, grew up in the church and have known him their
whole lives, but it was a matter of making their faith their own.
Some hit rock bottom using drugs or alcohol and had a come-to-
Jesus moment. For others, faith came through a relationship with a
friend, family member, or mentor who told them about Jesus. Maybe
it's a "moment in time" when someone prays a prayer and everything
changes. Or perhaps it's just a slow, gradual heart change. When I
talk to people, they tell me about surrendering their hearts to God,
then their minds to God, then maybe even their bodies to God . . .
but the last thing they let go of was their wallets. What I mean is,
full surrender in *every* area of their lives took much more time and
a lot more work.

For me, it was essentially the opposite. I had to learn how to trust God through my wallet first. I realize that's a bizarre way to go about it, but I believe with every fiber of my being that God meets us where we are. And, in 2010, that's where I was. I was consumed with thoughts about money. Every decision I made had financial implications. It was exhausting.

But from the moment I let go and began to trust him, everything changed. Once I focused on getting one area of my life healed and restored, every other area of my life started to heal too.

Now I want to be super clear about something. I am not over here telling you that if you cut a tithe check, you will suddenly start bathing in money. In no way, shape, or form do I believe in or espouse any kind of prosperity gospel.

The Bible does not say that if you become a Christian and give 10 percent of your money to the church that your life will suddenly be easy. Nope. Jesus doesn't promise that. Jesus promises a lot of other things.

- Matthew 11:28: He promises that if you are weary and burdened, he will give you rest.
- Deuteronomy 31:6: He promises he will never leave you nor forsake you.
- Romans 8:28: He promises that he will work *all* things together for the good of those who love him and are called according to his purpose.
- Isaiah 40:31: He promises to strengthen those who hope in him.
- James 1:12: He says that the one who endures trials is blessed, because when they have stood the test, they will receive the crown of life.

So no, I don't believe that if you treat the tithe like a compulsory box to check you'll automatically come into financial blessings. But what I *do* believe in is what happens on the other side of faith, obedience, and surrender—when the posture of your heart is so fixed on God that you can't help but put him first in every area of your life. Including your wallet.

For me, tithing wasn't something I began to do out of compulsion or guilt. Through obedience to God's Word, I believed I *had* to do it in order to radically change my heart posture. I had to give everything I had left. I had to go *all in* on Jesus.

A few weeks before I left for Kenya, John and I celebrated our "Toby-versary." Sure, Toby Keith wasn't the most romantic of first dates, but it was the date we recognized as the start of our relationship. (Even if we didn't admit to being boyfriend and girlfriend until Halloween.)

Two days *after* our anniversary, I came into work like I did every other day of the week. I was about to go on the air to do my daily "things around town" segment. I'd pop on to chat with the morning show host, Ron Stutts, to banter a bit, talk about what was new on the website, and update the community on events worth noting in the area.

Well, this particular day was going to be a little different. Patti Thorp, a good friend of mine (who also happened to be the wife of Holden Thorp, the chancellor at UNC–Chapel Hill at the time), popped into the studio and interrupted me *while* I was live on the air. Patti always had a bubbly spirit, but she was particularly cheerful on this occasion. After Patti showed up, Ken Jackson, the owner of a well-known jeweler in town called Wentworth & Sloan, also popped in and joined her in the commandeering of the WCHL airwaves. The next thing I knew, Patti and Ken were talking about someone's wedding.

The two of them excitedly rambling while Ron seemed to have no idea what was happening started to make me very suspicious. But John was nowhere to be seen, so I stood there clueless.

"But has the bride said yes yet?" Ken asked.

"Molly! Turn around!" yelled Patti excitedly.

I slowly turned, and through the glass window to the production studio behind me, John Stillman sat holding up a handwritten sign that said, "Will you go to the courthouse with me?" (Over the previous months, we had joked quite a bit about running down to the courthouse and getting married.)

I was in tears. Patti was in tears. Ken was in tears. Ron was so utterly confused because he had not been made aware that any of this was going to be happening on his show. The radio station phones were ringing off the hook. Everyone in the office was around the studio, clapping. People on the drive to work that morning got quite the audio experience.

John came around and got down on one knee, and I said yes! It was the most John Stillman way to propose. And we celebrated that day by going to lunch at Chipotle because we are very highbrow people.

For the next seven months, we planned the wedding on a shoestring budget. John's parents generously agreed to cover our rehearsal dinner and photographer, but we wanted to pay for everything else. I was still working hard to get out of debt, and both of us worked jobs with meager salaries. But we did it. We DIY-ed everything we could, and because we had so many relationships with vendors around town through our jobs at the radio station, we were able to get amazing deals on our food. My friends Bryan and Topher from college were our DJs, and my ridiculously talented sister, Bridgid, who owns an incredible bakery in Jamestown, North Carolina, gifted us the most beautiful *and delicious* wedding cake.

All the while, the most important thing to us was not allowing the stress or finances of the wedding to get in the way of starting our marriage off right. We made sure God was in every nook and cranny of our relationship from the get-go. I was hyper-aggressive about paying off debt at this point because, despite what John had told me about my burdens becoming our burdens and thus his burdens, I desperately did not want to bring my debt into our marriage. He'd been responsible with his money—bought a house at twenty-four years old, put 20 percent down, was debt-free, paid cash for cars . . . I knew that bringing my debt along would only add to the guilt I felt. Plus, I really wanted us to start our marriage with a clean slate. I was focused and determined.

We were getting married in February, and the entire week leading up to the wedding was cold, rainy, and downright disgusting weather. I was so worried that our wedding day would be gross. But when we woke up Saturday morning, it was beautiful. The sun was shining, and I kid you not, it was over sixty-five degrees when we started taking pictures before the ceremony. Unseasonably warm!

As I stood there looking in the mirror at myself in my gown and veil, I couldn't help but feel the tinge of a deep pain. I missed my mom so much. I missed her being there to help me pick out my dress, make the invitations, or arrange the flowers. My best friend Becca's mom came in and handed me the bouquet she'd made, and wrapped around the bouquet were my mom's dog tags from Vietnam and a little locket with her picture in it. I burst into tears and felt so grateful for this incredibly kind gesture.

The wedding was beautiful and the most fun (people *still* talk about how fun it was), and the next day, we woke up to freezing cold weather with *snow* on the ground. We couldn't help but believe our good fortune wasn't an accident.

We took a honeymoon to Mexico (using a LivingSocial deal and renting the cheapest car possible, a 1997 Chevrolet Chevy!*), and we came home a week later to start our life together as husband and wife. The next day, I wrote the last check to Novadebt, paying off every last cent of debt that I owed. I was debt-free! *We* were debt-free.

And we never looked back.

John left his job at the radio station and went to work for a financial advisor. Around this time I started taking my blog more seriously. While I was working a full-time job at the AV media company, I also spent many of my waking hours writing. I had no idea where it would take me, but I knew I loved to write and create, so I kept at it. Then, in the late fall of 2012, I found out I was pregnant with our first child. We were elated to be starting our family! On August 18, 2013, our daughter, Lilly, was born, and my life was forever changed, yet again. As I held that precious baby, I had flashes of what it must have felt like for my mom to hold me in her arms for the first time. I longed to ask her all the questions about motherhood. I longed for her to kiss me on the forehead and tell me I did it. I longed for her to say the words, "She's so beautiful."

In the fall of 2015, I was able to leave my day job to pursue blogging and writing full-time. John was experiencing some shifts of his own at work, and we felt called for him to go out and start an independent financial advisory firm. It was a terrifying leap of faith, but we knew God was asking us to be faithful to the thing in front of us.

---

* You may be thinking, *Molly, is this a typo? A Chevrolet "Chevy"?* And to you I say it is not, in fact, a typo. The Chevrolet Chevy was manufactured in Mexico from the mid-1990s until it was officially discontinued in 2012. It was manual transmission, drove like a nightmare, and the interior smelled like gasoline and cigarettes.

Within a span of four weeks, we both left our full-time, stable, health-insurance-providing day jobs to strike out on our own and become self-employed. Oh, did I mention that I was expecting our second child in a couple of months? Talk about a roller coaster. On February 19, 2016—one day after our four-year wedding anniversary—our son, Amos, was born.

The next few years were refining for us. We experienced some of the highest highs and some of the lowest lows. We were wrecked with grief by the loss of two sons, Elijah and Malachi, in the second trimester of pregnancy. We had business challenges, life challenges, friendship breakups, and a global pandemic, but we also grew in our faith and marriage more than ever before. Most of which is another story for another book.

But all of those things, every little step of the way, took us in the direction God had for us.

One thing I've failed to mention is that ever since John and I started dating, we'd talked about one day having a farm. We'd always say something like, "In ten years, let's buy land and build a house and start a farm." This was a frequent conversation for us.

In about 2015 or so, we started a savings account to earmark money for land. Every month we'd put money away. Some months it would be a little, some months it would be a lot. We didn't know what we'd do with it, but we thought we'd be consistent and faithful and let God lead.

In 2019, we *loosely* started looking around at land. We'd take the kids for drives and check out plots of land around us that might be good. But once again, the conversation would always go back to something along the lines of, "Ten years from now . . ." Even though we'd been saying that exact phrase for nine years at that point.

And then the COVID pandemic hit.

A switch flipped in us, and we knew God was calling us to do this. So, pretty quickly, we drove around more aggressively looking at land for sale. I can't even begin to tell you how many plots of land we walked. It was *so many*. We'd put offers in, only to get rejected. Or we'd put an offer in only to find out about some restrictive covenant that didn't allow animals. *You mean to tell me we can't even own* chickens *on this* ten acres of land*?! What!?*

We finally found a wooded, ten-acre property that felt like it was *the one*. We put in an offer, and it was accepted! But a few weeks into it, while under contract, we learned the land was in some sort of restricted watershed zone, which meant we couldn't clear any of the trees. Not having anywhere to grow food or pasture animals would create a bit of a challenge for farming. We had to back out of the contract, and we were crushed.

This went on for months.

Finally, after a conversation with a friend, we expanded our search to established homes on land or farm-type properties. Let's just say, this was not an easy search either. We looked at house after house, and nothing was "the one." We found one we thought was perfect, put in an offer, and lost out on it to someone else. The housing market was insane.

We had reached our wits' end. For sure, this was God telling us to give up. One Friday night, John came home from work and said, "I've had it! We can't search anymore. This is too much, and we need a break. We will try again in a year or two."

Two hours later, a house on over ten acres came on the market. It was white with black shutters, had a full-length covered front porch that partially wrapped around, had not one but two already-built barns, had a creek running through it, was in the exact area we wanted, and had zero restrictive covenants.

John and I looked at each other and said, "Do you see what I see? I think this is the one."

We went to look at it that weekend and knew before we'd even fully driven down the driveway that this was home. This was the farm we'd prayed for for ten years.

We put in an offer, and it was accepted the same day. We couldn't believe it. Selah Farm was born.

We always wanted more children, and if we'd had another girl, her name would have been Selah. *Selah* is a mysterious word in the Bible that has lost its true meaning in translation over the years, but in short, it means to rest, to breathe, and to reflect. We prayed that Selah Farm would be a place where people could rest, breathe, and reflect. A place where people would laugh, cry, and laugh 'til they cried.

As I sit here writing this very chapter, I hear my children outside running around and playing. I hear the crows of our roosters, the *bock bocks* of our chickens, the "buckwheats" of our guinea hens, and the bleats of our goats. I can see the fruit trees that will one day bring forth apples and pears and cherries for us to enjoy. I can see the beauty of the sunset over the trees—but I can't see our neighbors. (Nothing against them personally; I just want to be able to feed my chickens naked if I want to. I'm not *actually* going to feed my chickens while naked, but I want the freedom to do so, okay?)

Since we said "yes" to God and to this place, he's continued to blow us away. Our best friends moved into a house a mile away, my dad lives ten minutes from us, and we planted a church—we have found community that we prayed long and hard for. None of it has been easy, but we have been able to see and experience the body of Christ at work.

The thing I've learned is that if God is calling me to something, *even if it is terrifying*, I know he's going to be faithful. His promises are true. I trust him now more than ever before, and I can't wait to see what else he has in store.[†] I'm on this ride for the long haul.

Like the old hymn says, "I have decided to follow Jesus, no turnin' back, no turnin' back."

---

† Oh! That rhymed again!

22

IT IS FINISHED

NOW*

He said to me, "My grace is sufficient for you, for
my power is made perfect in weakness." Therefore I
will boast all the more gladly about my weaknesses,
so that Christ's power may rest on me. That is
why, for Christ's sake, I delight in weaknesses, in
insults, in hardships, in persecutions, in difficulties.
For when I am weak, then I am strong.

2 CORINTHIANS 12:9-10

Here we are. We've reached the end of the book. If you're still here, hooray! You did it! If I'm still here, it means I somehow finished writing this book, so I'm also going to pat myself on the back and say, "Hooray! I did it!" (That was very meta. I'm sorry.)

Like I mentioned way back in the beginning, this is my story. But, more honestly, it's God's story. It's a messy story, it's a muddy story, it's

---

* Now, as in the years of our Lord 2022 and 2023, when this chapter was composed and edited.

an honest story, it's a funny story, it's a sad story, and it's an unfinished story. Just like God's.

The fact is, I could live to be 137, or tomorrow I could take a fatal kick to the head from one of my goats (and I really hope that doesn't happen). I don't pretend to have it all together or have this life figured out. That would be ridiculous for me to say. But at my current ripe age of thirty-eight (as of this writing), I do have the benefit of hindsight that has taught me a lot.

For the first twenty-five years of my life, I didn't have God. So I did whatever I could to find the thing that could serve as my god. Tim Keller wrote a whole book on this idea called *Counterfeit Gods*, and you should read it. The idea is that all of us, whether we want to admit it or not, were created to worship *something*. And since we were created to worship our Creator God, if we don't worship him, then our hearts will just look for something else to give us a sense of significance, a sense of security, a sense of self-worth, a sense of happiness and joy, a sense of meaning. If our heart doesn't find identity in Christ, then our heart will find identity elsewhere. Whatever that thing is . . . *that* is an idol. An earthly idol. A counterfeit god.

Idol worship isn't necessarily some golden statue, a shrine we set up in our living room, or Kelly Clarkson. Idols are the things in our hearts that take the place of God—things like our love lives, careers, families, children, power, comfort, financial security, hotness, homes, the cars we drive, or the clothes we wear. In many ways, the idols themselves aren't the problem. They're simply things we are hoping will give us that which only God can give.

But, as idols always do, idols will break our hearts. And when an earthly idol disappoints us, we will react in basically one of four ways:

1. We blame the idol

2. We blame ourselves
3. We blame the world
    Or . . .
4. We realize we were created for something beyond this world

With the benefit of hindsight, I'm able to see so clearly that all I did for twenty-five years was worship counterfeit gods and seek after earthly idols.

For years I idolized the love my parents had for one another, so I did whatever I could to replicate that. I bounced from relationship to relationship, looking for the things only God could provide: love, identity, and self-worth. I looked for someone to love me unconditionally, despite my shortcomings. I looked for someone who would tell me what I wanted to hear. When each relationship failed, I'd blame the idol (he was the wrong guy) or myself (I'm the worst and it's no wonder he broke up with me).

I idolized the pursuit of success, achievement, power, and fame. I thought the only thing I'd ever want to do or be good at was to star on *Saturday Night Live*. After being voted "Class Clown" my senior year of high school, I was voted "Most Likely to Succeed" by my sorority in college. Clearly, this was my path! Sure, I was making people laugh . . . but I wasn't happy. So when my dreams of moving to New York were thwarted, when I couldn't get a job, when an improv show I was in bombed, or when I finally realized it was time to step away from comedy, I felt like I had no purpose. What good was I? Once again, I blamed the idol, and I blamed myself.

When I got a quarter-of-a-million-dollar inheritance, I went from having no money at my disposal to suddenly having a lot of it. I thought for sure that all this money would be my ticket to freedom. Money would get me what I wanted, and financial security would make everything all right. I watched my parents struggle financially for years and years and years. That wasn't going to be my story! Almost overnight, the money became central to my existence. I'd suddenly attained the thing I'd dreamt of in my wildest dreams, but every time I spent money, I'd just say, "What's next?" It was never enough. And then, when it was all gone, when I'd squandered every last penny, I blamed myself. In many ways, rightly so . . . It was my fault, after all.

When my mom got sick, I was too young to have the tools to process what I was seeing. The full, grim reality of her situation was hidden from me, so my mind was left to its own devices. In essence, I was merely seeing the outlines on a coloring page, and my mind filled in the rest with a combination of truth and untruth. I colored the apple red, but I colored the leaves on the trees hot pink. I was uncomfortable, so my idol became comfort—friendships, parental praise, and being a rock star in a Christian worship band called Doubting Thomas. I even tried to find comfort in my room in our house . . . I'd rearrange my furniture or move rooms whenever I was tired of things the way they were. Once again, it was something I could "control." And when the earthly search for comfort failed me, I blamed the world. "Well, my mom is sick and life sucks right now, so let's throw me a pity party." When she died, it only got worse. The world was out to get me, and I was destined for a life of pain and suffering.

When I sought earthly pleasure apart from God, my joy withered. I spent all my time looking for an alternate, pseudo-salvation in the things of this world rather than looking for the peace, freedom, salvation, and true joy that can only be found in Jesus. And so God did what he does—he used a really weird, roundabout way to get me to leave what was comfortable, to move to North Carolina, to bring me to my knees and way past my breaking point, to help me realize that all the things I'd been chasing and searching for . . . only he could give them to me.

Pain is a much greater teacher than blessing.

But God.

It took hitting rock bottom for me to discover that my identity is not found in making people laugh. It's found in showing people the source of real, true joy. And that I am not the hero of my story, God is.

I had to learn that my identity is not in the pursuit of my own power, fame, or glory. But it is found in the power of God within me, bringing fame and glory to his name, using the gifts I've been entrusted with to serve others, as a faithful steward "of God's grace in its various forms" (1 Peter 4:10).

I had to realize that I could not find comfort in financial security and that money, possessions, and worldly prosperity will only leave a person feeling empty and hollow. Money in and of itself is not evil; but the love and worship of money is. Through sacrificial giving, I learned that money is just a tool, and if stewarded well, it can be a powerful tool in building God's kingdom rather than my own earthly domain. I've learned this even more now as we've been on the journey of church planting.

I'm not saying I don't still fight a daily, if not hourly, battle with idols. I do. We *all* do. What it amounts to is a constant self-evaluation—a personal inventory I take of where I am placing my hope, my identity, and my self-worth. Because if I'm not seeking Christ every single day, then I'm hopeless. Without God, I am hopeless. There is absolutely nothing in this world that will bring me the lasting peace, hope, and freedom found in Jesus.

So now, when an earthly idol disappoints me—as they do and will only continue to—I have to react in that fourth way: to remember I was created for something beyond this earth. Theologian and writer C. S. Lewis famously put it this way in his book *Mere Christianity*: "If I find in myself a desire which no experience in this world can satisfy, the most probable explanation is that I was made for another world."

Dear reader, I have no idea where you are right now. I have no idea how or why you picked up this book. Did you intend to buy it, was it gifted to you, or did you find it in a bargain bin at Ollie's ("Good Stuff Cheap!") in the year 2078? I have no idea if you know Jesus, if you don't know Jesus, or if you once *thought* you knew Jesus but haven't been around him in a while.

As your friend—and I hope at this point in our journey together I can call you that—I want to lovingly say: He's there. He's waiting. Go after Jesus. Run after Jesus. Seek after Jesus. Whatever burden you're carrying, leave it at the feet of Jesus. Whatever shame you feel, let it go. Whatever earthly idol you're chasing, stop and chase after the One who knows you better than you know yourself.

Jesus. Jesus. Jesus.

"But *you* don't know *me*, Molly," you retort. "You don't know what I've done, you don't know what I've been through, you don't know the pain and hurt I've experienced, you don't know the thoughts I've thought or the things I've said, or [insert all the things I don't know here]."

You're right. I don't.

But God does. And he loves you anyway. He sent his Son to earth in the form of a helpless baby, to grow up, to show you the way to live, to take on your sin and your punishment, to die a horrible death on a cross for you, and to be raised from the dead three days later—declaring the final victory over it all. Whatever you think is too much for God, is not. All you have to do is go to him and say, "God, forgive me. I need you. Help me. I can't do this life without you. Restore that which is broken."

That's the first step. The rest of the healing process takes time—a lifetime, really.

I'm certainly further along in my journey than I was when I started. I guess that's the goal, isn't it? To be a little bit further along each day than we were the day before.

For the first eleven years I walked with Jesus, I knew I was forgiven. I knew in my heart of hearts that God had forgiven me. But it wasn't until January 2022 that I had a moment of clarity: I hadn't yet forgiven myself.

I was still carrying the weight of shame. The reason I kept the full truth and intimate details of my story a secret from everyone around me for so long was because I was ashamed. But suddenly I realized that my heavenly Father's work of forgiveness on the cross is finished. It's done. It's complete. All of *my* sins, all of *your* sins, were paid for by Jesus' death and resurrection. There's absolutely nothing I can add to that. There's nothing you can do to earn that. So how is it that I could receive the forgiveness God purchased for me with the blood of his Son and yet still walk around carrying the weight of guilt and shame? How are my standards of forgiveness holier and higher than God's? If God can forgive me, *who am I* to think I can't forgive myself?

My friend, if God can forgive you, who are you that you can't forgive yourself?

I can't promise life walking with the Lord will be easy. In fact, I can promise the opposite. Life is beautiful, but life is also so very hard. Jesus said, "I have told you these things, so that in me you may have peace. In this world you will have trouble. But take heart! I have overcome the world" (John 16:33). Notice that Jesus didn't say we *might* have trouble or that it *could* be cloudy with a chance of trouble. He said we *will* have trouble. It's a promise. A guarantee. Until we get to heaven or when Jesus comes back, whichever comes first, we will face suffering. Sometimes, life really sucks.

My mom used to say to me all the time that maturity is knowing that life isn't fair and learning to live with that. But it is also under-standing that on this side of heaven, we will never understand why some things happen or don't happen. The truth is, why does it matter? My mom spent years after Vietnam trying to figure out the *why*. I spent years after Mom died trying to figure out the *why*. But *why* can be a useless question. The better question is: What am I going to do now, and how can it make me a better person?

If all we do is focus on the hard or senseless parts of life, then we'll miss out on the joy and wonder God has for us. We can't forget that God himself invented it all. He's the inventor of joy, the inventor of beauty, the inventor of laughter, and the inventor of peace. We see that so clearly in the giggle of a baby, a beautiful sunset, or an ill-timed fart. Or a well-timed fart, for that matter. Hey, if you can't laugh at a fart, then you're missing out on a whole lot of life.

Dear reader, I'm praying for you right now. That God, in all his omniscience, will meet you right where you are. Farts and all.

ACKNOWLEDGMENTS

If you're reading this, then you are my people because I'm always the person who flips to the back of the book to read the thank-yous. Why? Because my Enneagram Two heart loves hearing about all the people that helped to make a book possible. And thus, I have actually somewhat dreaded writing the acknowledgments for my own book because I'm fearful I'm going to leave someone out or not thank someone *enough*. Because the truth is, this book 1,000 percent didn't happen without the help, support, prayers, and love of so many people. So with that, I'm going to do my best here.

First, thank you to the incredible Nelson Books team for how you have championed this book from the get-go. A secret I've kept from you until now: Nelson Books was my dream publisher. I never wanted to say it out loud because I didn't want to jinx it, but it truly has been an actual dream to work with you. Brigitta Nortker, you are a dream editor. I'm so glad you saw fit to choose me. Your sense of humor (case in point: you laughed *at* me when I fell the first time we met), your honesty, and your perfect execution of the compliment-sandwich have been exactly what I needed. This book is a better book because of you. Kathryn Duke, your attention to detail is a gift. You know that editing is easily my least favorite part of writing, but the way you guided me through the process has been exactly what I needed. John Andrade, Devin Duke, and Briá Woods—you are a marketing dream team. Thank you for how you have listened to my crazy ideas, celebrated with me, and dreamt big dreams with me. Your passion for this book means more to me than you will ever know. The biggest hugs and high fives to y'all.

I also have to give a special shoutout to Jenny Baumgartner. Jenny, as the editor who originally acquired this book, I can't thank you enough for believing in me and for seeing the potential in me and in this story. You gave me a chance and for that I am forever grateful.

To the Punchline Agency team members Amelia and Cynthia— thank you for all you do. Amelia, my book proposal was made stronger because of you. Cynthia, you have been such a cheerleader, and I adore you.

To Joy Eggerichs Reed, the dreamiest of dream agents. When I hit Send on that email to you asking you to be my agent back in 2021, I wanted to barf because I thought, *She's absolutely going to say no, and I will be devastated and unable to recover.* Little did I know you had stopped accepting new clients . . . and then you got my email. Joy, thank you for saying yes. I cried real, actual tears when you said yes. You take your job seriously, but you don't take yourself too seriously, and because of that, you are my favorite. Not only are you the best agent but you have become an even more incredible friend. Thank you for allowing me to send borderline inappropriate and unprofes- sional Marco Polos at all hours, thank you for allowing me to use your daughter's passport photo as a meme, and thank you for championing me along the way. I am a better writer and human being because I know you. I love you dearly. I also believe that we were absolutely separated at birth.

To the Third Wheel Media team, thank you for being way better at editing podcasts and writing show notes than I could ever be (or really than I try to be).

To my friends Ashley Abercrombie, Mary Marantz, Liz Bohannon, and Daniel Grothe—you were some of the earliest people I even mentioned that I was writing a book to, and you encouraged me every step of the way. Some of you even looked at my proposal early on and gave me feedback. You are doing the Lord's work in the world, and I am humbled to know each of you.

To Sharon Miller—Sharon, words will never capture my gratitude for you. You came into my life at one of my darkest times, and your friendship has been a balm to my soul. You not only have encouraged me through this entire book-writing journey, you have been a listening ear, you've been someone who can speak the truth in love to me, and you have challenged me. There's no one else on earth I'd rather go to Quincy, Illinois, with or sing "America the Beautiful" with as we cross the Mighty Mississippi or answer life-changing phone calls with. I'm a better person because I know you. I always tell people you're my smartest friend and I mean it. You are brilliant. You and Ike are so dear to me and there truly are not enough thank-yous in the world to accurately portray my gratitude for you.

Kim Butler, you are the coach of all coaches, and I'm so glad you're always in my corner. Thank you for believing in me, for celebrating with me, and for telling me to quit making excuses and do the hard thing.

To Steve Bezner, Sarah Delp, Bethany Scott, and the HNW family—you are deep wells of knowledge, joy, and edification. Thank you for how you've made me feel like part of the family even though I live states away. Thank you for introducing me to Lupe Tortilla and Pappacitos. While the Pappacitos garlic butter is clutch, Lupe (in my eyes) reigns supreme.

To Kristin Hannah, thank you. Thank you for how you bring a fresh voice to the stories of women that society overlooks. Thank you for how you use your experience and platform to elevate other women. Your grace, humility, and wisdom are a gift. You have no idea the impact you've had on my life, and I'm blown away that I can call you a friend. Thank you.

To my BSF sisters, I can say without a shadow of a doubt that I am who I am today in part because of you. You've given me a hunger for God's Word and shown me that only He can truly satisfy my every need and desire. You have equipped me, you have exhorted me, you have convicted me, you have led me, and you have changed me. I love you all dearly, and you're never going to get rid of me. May He increase as we decrease.

To my Generation Life Church family—what a ride of a lifetime we get to be on together, serving and saying yes to God and seeing the Holy Spirit move. You're beautiful. I love you so much.

To the Jazzagals—Meghan (and Wes), Amy (and Justin), Karla (and Derek), Glenda (and Charlie), Kimberly (and Aaron), and Libby (and Ryan)—I love y'all. Thank you for being the friends I prayed for. We have laughed together, wept together, and grown together. Thank you for being the true definition of iron sharpening iron. Thank you for being the friends who I know are up for any excuse to whip up an award-worthy charcuterie board.

Dave and Kristin—"Jerry is annoyed when Elaine keeps using his bonus room to write her manuscript because her 'internet keeps going out.' Kramer is miffed when he isn't properly thanked in the acknowledgments." I love you both so much, and I'm really glad that you're the only people who will understand this reference. Feel free to use it in season 6.

Abbi and Emma—I can't possibly Google enough synonyms for

thank you to accurately express my love for you two. Emma, thanks for letting me be your "second mom." It's the honor of a lifetime to watch you grow up. You're an incredible young woman (now young adult), and I love you. Abbi, my sister from another mister. I don't know what I'd do without you.

To John and Gretta—thank you for being the most incredible in-laws and for how you welcomed me into your family. Thank you for generously allowing me to go to LLH and OKI to write, thank you for how you're the best Papa and Bomma to our kids, and thank you for raising the most incredible husband. You exemplify what a loving, Christ-like marriage should be. I love you.

Bob and Kyle, thank you for being the best brother-in-law and nephew a gal could ask for. Thank you for loving my sister so well.

Bridgid, I'm so glad that I get to call you my sister. You are brave, beautiful, and kind. Life has been beautiful and brutal for us both, and we are stronger on the other side. I thought of you nearly every moment while writing these words, and I pray you feel that. I love you so much, more than words can express.

Dad, I'm sorry if I was ever a mouthy toddler or an ignorant teenager. I'm sorry I didn't ask the questions I should have asked sooner. Thank you for having the hard conversations with me. Thank you for loving Mom so well and being the shining example of "till death us do part." Thank you for bringing Cindy into our lives to show us what love-after-death can look like. (PS I love you, Cindy!) Thank you for teaching me to see the humor in even the darkest of moments. You are the best dad a girl could ask for, and I love you oh so much.

Lilly and Amos, I'm so glad God saw fit to make me your mama. I pray that when you're old enough to read this book *and* understand it, that you see that your mama is just an imperfect woman chasing after a perfect Savior. I pray that you know there is beauty in our brokenness, and I pray that you learn from my mistakes. I know you will make mistakes of your own, and I pray that you know that your loving Heavenly Father will always be there to pick you right back up when you inevitably fall. I love you to the moon and back.

John, I know you loathe public acknowledgments, but this is my book so I'm going to do what I want. That cold December day when I showed you my bank statements, I thought for sure you were going to run for the hills, but instead you showed me what unconditional love could look like. While you may want to "look like you could be security" at any given moment, the man I know is so much more than that. You have the most generous heart of anyone I know. I see you when no one else does, and I see how you chase after God with all that you are. You are a man of integrity, and there's no one in the world that I trust more than you. Thank you for loving me, for being my biggest fan, and for rubbing my feet anytime I ask. Building our life together is a dream. You are also really hot. Thanks for marrying me, you didn't have to do that.

To anyone else in my life that I didn't explicitly name in this section (especially those of you who are in this book), please know that I love you, you know who you are, and thank you for being a part of my life. This section is already way longer than my publisher wants it to be, so I have to end somewhere.

Lastly, to Jesus (yes, I'm thanking Jesus here). I want to know You more. I want to love You more. And I pray that You have shone through every word on these pages . . . even the ugly and messy ones. I am who I am today because of You.

To God be the glory.